【漢英對照】

[CHINESE-ENGLISH
BILINGUAL EDITION]

論語今譯

THE ANALECTS OF CONFUCIUS

今譯　楊伯峻　吴樹平
英譯　潘富恩　温少霞

Modern Chinese Translation
by Yang Bojun & Wu Shuping
English Translation by
Pan Fuen & Wen Shaoxia

齊魯書社
Qi Lu Press

前　言

《論語》這一書名，有它特定的含義。根據班固《漢書·藝文志》的記載，“論”是“論纂”的意思，“語”是“語言”的意思。孔子在日常生活和執教過程中，發表過許多言論，他的弟子也有不少言論。“論語”就是把這些言論論纂起來的意思。實際上，《論語》所載，不限於孔子及其弟子的言論，也包括了他們不少的社會實踐活動。也就是說，書中既記言，又載行。

《論語》共二十篇，每篇由若干章組成。這些篇章排列的先後，并沒有內在的聯系。即使前後兩章之間，也沒有什麼關連。而且，書中多次出現重複的章節。有些重複章節字句完全相同。如“巧言令色鮮矣仁”一章，先見於《學而篇》，又見於《陽貨篇》。還有的不同章節，只是文字詳略不同。如“君子不重”章，《學而篇》比《子罕篇》多出十一字，其他文字相同。另外，還有一些章節意思相同，記載有異。如《憲問篇》說：“不患人之不己知，患其不能也。”《衛靈公篇》又說：“君子病無能焉，不病人之不己知也。”兩章意思完全相同。從這些現象可以斷定，《論語》一書，不是由一個人編輯。大多數研究者認為，《論語》是在孔子死後，由孔子弟子和再傳弟子在不同時期撰輯而成的。

孔子名丘，字仲尼，魯國陬邑（今山東曲阜）人。生於魯襄公二十二年（公元前551年），也有人認為生於魯襄公二十一年，死於魯哀公十六年（公元前479年）。據孔子自己所說，他是殷商苗裔。周武王滅了殷商，封殷商的微子啟於宋。孔子的先祖孔父嘉是宋國宗室，因為距離宋國始祖已經超過五代，便改為孔氏。孔父嘉的後代防叔畏懼華氏的逼迫出奔到魯國，防叔生伯夏，伯夏生叔梁紇，叔梁紇生孔子。

孔子幼年喪父，家境中落。年輕時曾管理倉庫，看管牛羊。他勤於學習，博學多能。三十多歲時，開始講學授徒，打破了“學在官府”的傳統。魯定公九年（公元前501年），出任魯國中都宰，遷升為司空，又官大司寇。五十四歲時，代理宰相三個月。當時，魯定公和執政的季桓子接受齊國女樂，怠於政事，孔子復興周禮的抱負難以實現，他便帶領弟子周游列國，前後長達十四年。他先後到過衛、陳、曹、宋、鄭、蔡、楚等國，都沒有受到重用。魯哀公十一年（公元前484年），季康子以幣迎孔子，孔子返回魯國。這時，孔子已經六十八歲了。返魯後，他把主要精力投入到教育方面，又致力于整理《詩》、《書》、《易》等古代典籍，刪修《春秋》。

孔子所處的春秋時代，是奴隸制向封建制過渡的時期，諸侯兼併，戰爭頻仍，禮崩樂壞。為了變革社會現實，他建立了寬博宏大的思想體系。這一思想體系，主要保存在《論語》一書中。

從《論語》中可以看出，“仁”是孔子思想體系的核心。所謂“仁”，用孔子的話來說就是“愛人”。當然，對“仁”的理解不能過于狹窄，它有廣闊的內涵。“克己復禮為仁”，“能行五者（恭、寬、信、敏、惠）於天下為仁”，“己欲立而立人，己欲達而達人”也是“仁”。推己及人的忠恕之道，可以說是“仁”的核心，所以曾子有言：“夫子之道，忠恕而已矣。”“忠恕”與“愛人”是一致的。

從“仁”的主張出發，在政治上，孔子要求實行德政，重視教化，刑罰寬弛，經濟上惠民，使民“足食”。為了把德政變為現實，孔子主張舉拔賢人。

對待天命的認識，孔子繼承了原始宗教的天命觀，肯定了天的人格神地位。他承認，他的個人品德，肩負的使命，乃至個人的生死和社會治亂，都離不開天命。所以君子有三畏，“畏天命”居於首位。在他看來，“不知命，無以為君子”。但在天命面前，孔子反對消沉，主張順應天命，有所作為。孔子一方面相信天命，另一方面又不贊同利用卜筮探求天意，對鬼神也采取敬而遠之的態度，既不相信，也不否定。這與傳統的觀念有所不同。

孔子在長期的教育實踐中，提出了許多教育主張。"有教無類"是他收取學生的原則，這就使過去沒有資格接受教育的基層平民，得到了受教育的機會。這種思想的形成，與他早年卑微貧困的處境不無關系。孔子教育學生的最終歸宿，是讓他們出來作官從政。在教育方法上，他主張"學而時習之"，溫故知新；提倡因材施教，教育內容因人而異；強調"知之為知之，不知為不知"，老老實實地學習；主張治學先要立人，強調品德的重要性。

孔子的思想在中國歷史上影響極大。自漢武帝罷黜百家，獨尊儒術以後，確立了孔子思想的全尊地位。他的思想影響滲透到中國歷史的每一個領域。今天，不論是研究孔子，還是研究中國歷史，都離不開《論語》。它在封建社會被尊崇為經典，是每一個學子的必讀之書。我們把它翻譯成現代語體文，會給學習《論語》的讀者帶來一些方便。

楊伯峻以前撰寫了《論語譯注》，由中華書局出版。又撰寫了《白話四書》，內有《論語》譯文。這次翻譯《論語》，是在楊伯峻的兩個譯本基礎上修訂而成。修訂工作由吳樹平獨力完成。

MODERN CHINESE TRANSLATOR'S PREFACE

The name of this book, *Lun Yü* (The Analects of Confucius), has its own particular meaning. According to Ban Gu's The History of the Han Dynasty, the character Lun means editing and Yü means speeches. Confucius made many speeches in everyday life and in the course of his teaching activities, and so did his disciples. Lun Yü thus means edited speeches. As a matter of fact, this book records the speeches made by Confucius and his disciples and also includes their social practice. In other words, the book records both speeches and conduct.

The Analects of Confucius consists of 20 books with a number of chapters in each. There is no internal order in their arrangement and there is even no relationship between the adjacent chapters. Morever, there are chapters that reappear a number of times. Some of them are completely the same, for example, the chapter of "Honey words and flattering looks seldom speak of human-heartedness" first appears in BOOK I XUE ER, and then reappears in BOOK XVII YANG HUO. Some chapters reappear in different words and length, for example, the chapter of "A superior man , if he is not grave…" first appears in BOOK I XUE ER, but when it reappears in BOOK IX ZI HAN, it is 11 characters longer, whereas the rest of it is the same. Besides, some chapters share the same meaning but they are presented in different forms, for example, the chapter of "I'm not concerned at men's not knowing me, I'm concerned at my own want of ability." in BOOK XIV XIAN WEN and the chapter of "A superior man is distressed by his own want of ability. He is not distressed by other's not knowing him." in BOOK XV WEI LING GONG are of the same meaning. It might therefore concluded that the Analects of Confucius was not compiled by one person, but was, as most researchers agree, compiled by several of Confucius' disciples and their own disciples, at different times after his death.

Confucius' name is Qiu, his personal name Zhongni. He was born in Zuo County of the state of Lu (today's Qufu County, Shandong Province) in the 22nd year of the reign of Duke Xiang of Lu (551 B. C., or in the 21st year of this reign, believed by others.) and died in the 16th year of the reign of Duke Ai of Lu (479 B. C.). He said, he was the descendant of the imperial family of Shang Dynasty. After King Wu of Zhou overthrew the Shang Dynasty, Wei Zi, a member of the imperial family of Shang Dynasty, was made the prince of Song. Confucius' ancestor, Kong Fujia, was the imperial clansman of the State of Song. It was from Kong Fujia that the new surname of his family was taken since he was five generations later than the ancestors in the State of Song. Kong Fujia's descendant Fangshu went to the State of Lu to seek refuge from Hua's intrigues. Fangshu gave birth to Boxia, and from him came Shuliang He, the father of Confucius.

When Confucius was very young his father died and so he

suffered a fall in his family fortune. As a young man, he made a living by looking after cattle and sheep. He was very diligent in learning and he became very learned and versatile. In his thirties, he began to recruit and lecture disciples, which broke the convention that "education must be monopolized by the government". Confucius took the post of the senior official of Zhongdu in the 9th year of the reign of Duke Ding of Lu (501 B. C.)and was promoted to minister of public affairs and minister of crimes, later. At the age of 54, he acted for the Prime Minister for three months, At that time, Duke Ding of Lu and the governor Ji Huan Zi neglected state affairs and indulged in sensual pleasures. Finding it impossidle to realize his ambition---the revival of the Zhou Dynasty's rituals. Confucius set off on 14 years' travels through various states such as Wei , Chen, Cao , Song, Zhen, Cai and Chu, but he was not assigned to a high post in any of these places. In the 11th year of the reign of Duke Ai of Lu(484 B. C.)he returned to Lu and was welcomed and given gifts from Ji Kang Zi. At that time Confucius was over 68 years old . After his return to Lu, he was fully engaged in education and he collated the classics such as the Book of Poetry, the Book of History and the Book of Changes and he revised the Spring and Autumn Annals.

Confucius lived in the Spring and Autumn Period, which was a transition period from slavery to feudalism. Vassals annexed territories from each other, wars broke out frequently and there was decline in social morality. To reform society, Confucius established a grand system of thinking, which was mainly contained in the Analects of Confucius.

It can be seen in this book that Ren (human-heartedness or perfect virtue) is central in his system of thinking. Ren, in his own words, is "to love people". Ren, of course, should not be understood in too narrow a sense since it suggests a much wider connotation. "To subdue one's-self and turn to propriety is perfect virtue." "He who can put five things (gravity, open-heartedness, sincerity, earnest and kindness) into practice everywhere under heaven is a man of perfect virtue." "Desiring to sustain himself, sustains others; desiring to develop himself, develops others" is also Ren. Confucius himself put himself in the place of another and this kind of Zhong (loyalty) and Shu (consideration) could be considered as the core of Ren. Zen Zi said, "The Master's teaching consists of the principle of loyalty and consideraion, and that is all." Zhong and Shu are consistent with "loving people".

From the viewpoint of Ren, what Confucius advocated on politics were: governing by virtue, emphasis on education, mitigation of severe punishment; and what he advocated on economy were: benefiting people and supplying them with sufficient food. In order to put governing by virtue into practice, he suggested selecting and promoting the talents and virtue.

Regarding the will of Heaven, Confucius inherited the views from those of primitive religion which held Heaven as the Deity. He accepted that his personality, his mission, even his life and death, and the social order are all in control of the will of Heaven. Therefore, there were three things of which a superior man stood in awe, and above all else he stood in awe of the will of Heaven. In his opinion, "he who does not know the will of Heaven cannot be a superior man. "But Confucius opposed submitting to the will of Heaven. Instead, he advocated obedience to the will of Heaven and living with a positive aim. Confucius believed in the will of Heaven, but on the other hand, he also was against divining and advocated a reverent and timid attitude toward the spirits and gods, which he neither believed in nor denied. This differs from the conventional ideas of the time.

In the course of his teaching over a long period, Confucius put forward lots of views on education. In recruiting disciples, he followed the guideline "Education recognizes no castes", which, as a result, provided opportunities for the common people to be educated. These people had no right to get an education in the past. These ideas were largerly fostered by the humbleness and poverty that Confucius suffered when he was young. The ultimate goal of his teaching was to prepare students for posts in the government. In respect of the teaching methods, he suggested that "One should learn and review constantly one has learned". He thought that by reviewing old knowledge one gains new knowledge. He proposed that students should be taught according to their aptitude and that teaching material should be student-based. He insisted that "say you know it when you know a thing and admit you do not know it when you do not know a thing"---an honest attitude to learning. He put self-cultivation before study and he emphasized the moral sense.

Confucius' doctrines had great influence on Chinese history. Han Wudi rejected other schools of thoughts but held Confucianism in esteem and so its leading position in Chinese history was established. Its influence was so extensive in China that the Analacts of Confucius is indispensable even now, either for studies on Confucius himself or for studies in Chinese history. The Analects of Confucius was worshipped as a classic in the period of the feudal society and every scholar was required to read it. We have translated it into modern Chinese in the hope that it may be of some convenience to those who study it.

This book is a revised version based on Yang Bojun's two versions: Analects of Confucius with Translation and Annotation(published by Zhonghua Publishing House), and a Modern Chinese Version of Four Books, which contains the Analects of Confucius. This modern Chinese edition was revised by Wu Shuping.

英譯説明

《論語》是中國人的聖經。

在數千年的歷史長河中，孔子思想對中國社會、文化乃至民族心理結構等各方面發生了非常深刻而廣泛的影響；而且，孔子思想還跨出了國界，在東亞文化圈中居主導地位，可以說，沒有孔子思想，東亞文明便不成其為東亞文明了；不僅如此，孔子思想對整個世界的影響也是舉世矚目的，人們已把孔子作為改變世界面貌的思想家之一。孔子思想主要記載在《論語》一書里。孔子思想對中國的影響，主要靠一部《論語》；其對東亞的影響，主要靠一部《論語》；其對世界的影響，還是主要靠一部《論語》。

人們普遍認為，在未來世界文化中，孔子思想將繼續扮演一個重要角色。這仍然要靠一部《論語》。

由於《論語》的特殊歷史地位，歷代都有大批的《論語》研究者和注釋者。在古代，最經典的注本是朱熹的《論語集注》；在當代，較權威的注本為楊伯峻的《論語譯注》；如今，吳樹平又在楊氏譯注的基礎上加以修訂，這就進一步提高了其學術價值。

《論語》的英文全譯本自上世紀中葉就出現了；其後，又有多種譯本問世。遺憾的是，目前反映當代中國《論語》研究成果的《論語》英譯本還不多見。正是為了彌補這個不足，我們以吳樹平修訂的今譯本為根據將《論語》譯成英文，同時兼採國外的《論語》研究成果，參考了 James Legge 的 Confucian Analects, Leonard A. Lyall 的 The Sayings of Confucius 和 Arthur Waley 的 The Analects of Confucius 等譯本。

在翻譯過程中我們發現，由於文化的差異，孔子思想的許多重要概念在英語中很難找到對應的詞，我們只能以大致相當的詞譯之，而在其首次出現時於括號中標上漢語拼音；其次，《論語》各篇篇名，不過是摘取每篇開頭幾個重要字眼來命名的，並無其它意義，故翻譯時只能以漢語拼音標之；另外，為了便於理解，我們在必要的地方作了少量注解。特此說明。

本書全部英文稿譯出後，承亞洲語言與研究中心聯席主席 Colin Mackerras 教授和來自美國 Beloit 大學的復旦大學留學生 Jona Thaw Levitt 先生認真作了審校，謹在此深致謝忱！

譯文不足之處，願受教焉。

ENGLISH TRANSLATOR'S NOTE

The position of the Analects of Confucius in Chinese culture is just like that of the Bible in western culture.

For thousands of years, Confucianism has exerted a far-reaching influence on Chinese society, culture and on the Chinese psychology. Its influence has extended abroad and Confucianism has held a leading position in the East Asian Cultural Circles. It might be said that East Asian Civilization would not come into being without Confucianism. What is more, its influence on the whole world is apparent since Confucius is considered as one of the greatest thinkers who have changed the world. Confucian doctrines are mainly recorded in the Analects of Confucius. Its influence on China is maintained by the Analects of Confucius; its influence on East Asia is maintained by the Analects of Confucius; its influence on the world is maintained by the Analects of Confucius, too.

It is generally acknowledged that Confucianism will continue to play an important role in the world culture in the future, and this still would be based on the Analects of Confucius.

Owing to its special historical significance, there have been a large number of researchers and annotators of the

Analects of Confucius in different periods. In ancient times, Zhu Xi's the Annotated Analects of Confucius was considered as a classic in annotating the Analects of Confucius, whilst in the modern period Yang Bojun's the Analects of Confucius with Translation and Annotation would be considered more authoritative. Now Wu Shuping has improved its academic value by his revised version based on Yang Bojun's annotations.

The first complete English version of the Analects of Confucius was made in the middle of the last century, after which there were a number of different English versions. It is a pity that there are now few English versions which reflect the results of contemporary researches on the Analects of Confucius in China. Therefore we have done service by once again translating the Analects of Confucius into English. This English version is made from Wu Shuping's revised version, with reference to Confucian Analects by James Legge, the Sayings of Confucius by Leoard A. Lyall and the Analects of Confucius by Arthur Waley.

In the course of translating this book, we have found it difficult to render many important concepts of Confucianism exactly into English because of the cultural differences. Therefore they have been rendered in an approximation of their literal meaning, with Pinyin in place of Chinese characters in the brackets for the terms that appear for the first time. As for the titles of each book in the Analects of Confucius, they are merely a few important Chinese characters in the first sentence of each book. They have no specific meaning. So we just put them into Pinyin. We have made some notes when necessary for further understanding.

We are greatly indebted to Professor Colin Mackerras, co-director of the Key Centre for Asian Languages and Studies, and to Mr. Jona Thaw Levitt, an exchange student from Beloit College in the U. S. A., and is now at Fudan University. They took the trouble to read through the English manuscript and carefully correct it. They helped us in polishing the languge.

Needless to say, there are some inadequacies in this book. Any suggestions or comments are welcome.

目　錄

CONTENTS

論語今譯

（漢英對照）

THE ANALECTS OF CONFUCIUS

(CHINESE-ENGLISH BILINGUAL EDITION)

學而篇第一

1·1　子曰:"學而時習之,不亦説乎？有朋自遠方來,不亦樂乎？人不知而不愠,不亦君子乎？"

【譯文】孔子說:"學到了知識,并時時復習,不是很愉快嗎？有志同道合的人從遠方來,不是很快樂嗎？人家不了解我,我卻不怨恨,不是道德高尚的君子嗎？"

1·2　有子曰:"其爲人也孝弟,而好犯上者,鮮矣;不好犯上,而好作亂者,未之有也。君子務本,本立而道生。孝弟也者,其爲仁之本與!"

【譯文】有子說:"他為人孝順父母,敬愛兄長,卻喜歡觸犯上級,這種情況是很少的;不喜歡觸犯上級,卻喜歡反叛作亂,這種情況是沒有的。君子致力於根本,根本樹立了,道就會由此而生。孝順父母,敬愛兄長,就是'仁'的根本吧!"

1·3　子曰:"巧言令色,鮮矣仁!"

【譯文】孔子說:"花言巧語,一臉媚色,這種人,'仁'就很少了。"

1·4　曾子曰:"吾日三省吾身——爲人謀而不忠乎？與朋友交而不信乎？傳不習乎？"

【譯文】曾子說:"我每天多次反躬自問替別人辦事,是不是盡心竭力了呢？同朋友交往,是不是誠心實意呢？老師傳授我的

BOOK I XUE ER

1.1 The Master said, "Is it not pleasant to learn and to review constantly what one has learned? Is it not delightful to have friends coming from afar? Is he not a superior man, who feels no discontent though others do not know him?"

1.2 You Zi[1] said, "There are few who are filial and fraternal but like to offend against their superiors. There have been none who do not like to offend against their superiors but like to rebel. The superior man works upon the root. When the root is taken, the Way (Dao) naturally grows. Filial piety and fraternal submission! —are they not the root of human heartedness (Ren)?"

1.3 The Master said, "Honey words and flattering looks seldom speak of human-heartedness."

1.4 Zeng Zi[2] said, "I daily examine myself for several times: have I been conscientious in working for others? Have I been sincere in dealings with friends? Have I reviewed what my

---

① i.e. You Ruo, a disciple of Confucius.

② A disciple of Confucius.

學業,是不是復習了呢?”

1·5 子曰:“道千乘之國,敬事而信,節用而愛人,使民以時。”

【譯文】孔子說:“治理擁有一千輛兵車的國家,要嚴肅認真地處理政事,誠信無欺,節約費用,愛護人民,農閑時役使老百姓。”

1·6 子曰:“弟子入則孝,出則悌,謹而信,汎愛衆而親仁。行有餘力,則以學文。”

【譯文】孔子說:“後生小子在父母跟前,便孝順父母;離開自己住室,便敬愛兄長;說話謹慎誠實可信,博愛大衆,親近有仁德的人。有多餘的力量,就去學習文獻。”

1·7 子夏曰:“賢賢易色;事父母,能竭其力;事君,能致其身;與朋友交,言而有信。雖曰未學,吾必謂之學矣。”

【譯文】子夏說:“(對待妻子,)重視品德,不重容貌;侍奉父母,能夠竭心盡力;侍奉君王,能夠獻身;同朋友交往,說話誠實守信。(這種人,)雖說沒有學習過,我一定說他是已經學習過了。”

1·8 子曰:“君子不重,則不威,學則不固。主忠信。無友不如己者。過則勿憚改。”

【譯文】孔子說:“君子不莊重,就沒有威望,即使學習,也不會把所學的知識鞏固下來。要以忠和信兩種品德為主。不要同不如自己的人交朋友。有了過錯就不要怕改正。”

1·9 曾子曰:“慎終追遠,民德歸厚矣。”

teacher taught me?"

1.5 The Master said, "To rule a country of a thousand chariots, the ruler should attend strictly to business, keep his promises, economize in expenditure, love the people, and use the labour of the peasantry at the proper seasons."

1.6 The Master said, "A youth should be filial at home and respectful to his elders abroad. He should be cautious and truthful. He should love all and cultivate the friendship of the virtuous. When he still has time and energy after having done all these, he should study the cultural heritage."

1.7 Zixia① said, "If a man honours his wife's virtue and withdraw his mind from her beauty; if he can exert his utmost strength to serve his parents; if he can devote his life to serve his prince; if he speaks sincerely in his dealings with his friends:—such a man, although men say that he has not learned, I will ccertainly say that he has."

1.8 The Master said, "A superior man, if he is not grave, he will not get any respect, and his learning will not be sound. He should hold faithfulness and sincerity as first principles. He should not make friends with those who are not as good as him. When he has faults, he must not fear to correct them."

1.9 Zeng Zi said, "Pay a careful attention to the funeral

---

① A disciple of Confucius.

【譯文】曾子說："謹慎地對待父母的去世，追念遠代的祖宗，（這樣做，）百姓的道德風尚就趨於忠厚了。"

1·10 子禽問于子貢曰："夫子至於是邦也，必聞其政，求之與？抑與之與？"子貢曰："夫子溫、良、恭、儉、讓以得之。夫子之求之也，其諸異乎人之求之與？"

【譯文】子禽問子貢說："先生到了一個國家，一定能了解到那個國家的政治情況，是自己打聽來的呢？還是別人告訴他的呢？"子貢說："先生是靠溫和、善良、嚴肅、節儉、謙遜而得來的。先生這種獲得的方法，不同於別人獲得的方法吧？"

1·11 子曰："父在觀其志，父沒觀其行，三年無改於父之道，可謂孝矣。"

【譯文】孔子說："父親在世時便觀察他的志向，父親去世後便考察他的行為，如果三年不改變父親的所為，可以說是孝了。"

1·12 有子曰："禮之用，和爲貴。先王之道，斯爲美，小大由之。有所不行，知和而和，不以禮節之，亦不可行也。"

【譯文】有子說："禮的運用，以和諧為可貴。先王治國之道的好處正在這里，不論小事、大事都照這樣去做。但也有不能這樣做的。只知道要和諧而一意求和諧，不用禮節來節制，也是不可行的。"

1·13 有子曰："信近於義，言可復也。恭近於禮，遠恥辱也。因不失其親，亦可宗也。"

【譯文】有子說："說話有信用而近於義，說的話就能兌現。態度恭敬而近于禮，就能不遭受耻辱。所依靠的是關係密切的人，也就靠得住了。"

rites to parents, recall forefathers, then the virtue of the people will resume its proper excellence."

1. 10 Ziqin[①] asked Zigong[②], "When our Master comes to a country, he is sure to learn its government affairs. Does he ask the information himself or is it offered to him?" Zigong replied, "Our Master is benign, upright, courteous, temperate, and complaisant, and thus he gets the information. Is the Master's way of enquiring not different from that of others?"

1. 11 The Master said, "While a man's father is alive, look at his intentions; when his father is dead, look at his conduct. If for three years he does not alter from the way of his father, he may be called filial."

1. 12 You Zi said, "In practising the rules of propriety, it is harmony that is prized. This is what is so precious in the ways of the ancient kings. They followed this principle in things small and great. Yet it is not to be observed in all cases. To know how such harmony should be prized, yet manifest it without regulating it by the rules of propriety, is something which should not be done."

1. 13 You Zi said, "If promises are made according to righteousness (Yi), words can be fulfilled; if respect is shown according to propriety, shame can be kept at bay. If one relies on intimates, he can be trusted."

---

① i. e. Cheng Kang. Some historians consider him as a disciple of Confucius.
② A disciple of Confucius.

1·14 “子曰:君子食無求飽,居無求安,敏於事而慎於言,就有道而正焉,可謂好學也已。”

【譯文】孔子說:“君子吃飯不求飽腹,居住不求舒適,對工作勤勞敏捷,說話小心謹慎,到有道的人那裏去匡正自己,這樣可以說是好學了。”

1·15 子貢曰:“貧而無諂,富而無驕,何如?”子曰:“可也。未若貧而樂,富而好禮者也。”

子貢曰:“《詩》云:‘如切如磋,如琢如磨’,其斯之謂與?”子曰:“賜也,始可與言《詩》已矣,告諸往而知來者。”

【譯文】子貢說:“貧窮卻不巴結奉承,富有卻不驕傲自大,(這種人)怎麽樣?”孔子說:“可以了,但還不如貧窮卻樂於道,富有而喜好禮的人。”

子貢說:“《詩經》上說:‘像對待骨、角、象牙、玉石一樣,先切削,再銼平,然後精雕細刻,進行磨光。’大概就是您說的這個意思吧?”孔子說:“賜啊,現在可以和你討論《詩經》了。(你能舉一反三,)告訴你過去的事,就能推知未來的事。”

1·16 子曰:“不患人之不己知,患不知人也。”

【譯文】孔子說:“不怕別人不了解自己,只怕自己不了解別人。”

爲政篇第二

2·1 子曰:“爲政以德,譬如北辰居其所而衆星共之。”

【譯文】孔子說:“用道德來治理政事,就會像北極星一樣,安居在自己的位置上,別的星辰都環繞着它。”

1. 14 The Master said, "A superior man does not seek satiety in his food nor ease in his dwelling-place. He is earnest in what he is doing and cautious in his speech. He associates with those who possess the Way and thereby he may be rectified. Such a person may indeed be said to love learning."

1. 15 Zigong said, "Poor, but no flatterer; rich, but not proud. What do you think of that?" The master said, "It will do, but better still is the man who, though poor, yet delighting in the Way; or the man who, though rich, loves the rules of propriety."

Zigong said, "It is said in the Book of Poetry: 'As you cut and then file, as you carve and then polish.' The meaning is the same, I suppose, with what you have just said." The Master said, "Ci①, with you I can begin to talk about the Book of Poetry. When I told you one point, you know its proper sequence."

1. 16 The Master said, "I do not worry about others not knowing me; what I worry about is that I do not know others."

BOOK II WEI ZHENG

2. 1 The Master said, "He who rules by means of his virtue is like the north polar star, which remains in its place and all the other stars turn towards it."

---

① i. e. Zigong.

2·2　子曰："《詩》三百，一言以蔽之，曰：'思無邪。'"

【譯文】孔子說："《詩經》三百篇，用一句話來概括它，就是'思想没有邪念'。"

2·3　子曰："道之以政，齊之以刑，民免而無恥。道之以德，齊之以禮，有恥且格。"

【譯文】孔子說："用政令來誘導，用刑罰來整治，百姓只是暫時地不犯罪，卻没有羞耻之心。用道德來誘導，用禮教來整治，百姓不但有羞恥之心，而且言行都歸於正道。"

2·4　子曰："吾十有五而志于學，三十而立，四十而不惑，五十而知天命，六十而耳順，七十而從心所欲，不踰矩。"

【譯文】孔子說："我十五歲立志學習，三十歲能自立，四十歲不會被迷惑，五十歲能知天命，六十歲對聽到的事情能分辨真假，判明是非，七十歲便隨心所欲，不離準則。"

2·5　孟懿子問孝。子曰："無違。"

樊遲御，子告之曰："孟孫問孝於我，我對曰，無違。"樊遲曰："何謂也？"子曰："生事之以禮，死葬之以禮，祭之以禮。"

【譯文】孟懿子問孔子怎樣才是孝。孔子說："不要違背禮節。"

樊遲替孔子駕車，孔子告訴他說："孟孫問我怎樣才是孝，我回答說，不要違背禮節。"樊遲說："這是什麼意思？"孔子說："父母活着，按照禮節侍奉他們；死了，按照禮節埋葬他們，按照禮節祭祀他們。"

2·6　孟武伯問孝。子曰："父母唯其疾之憂。"

【譯文】孟武伯問孔子什麽是孝。孔子說："要讓你的父母只

2. 2 The Master said, "In the Book of Poetry there are three hundred poems. But the essence of them can be covered in one sentence: 'Have no depraved thoughts.' "

2. 3 The Master said, "If the people are guided by law, and kept in order by punishment, they may try to avoid crime, but have no sense of shame. If they are guided by virtue, and kept in order by the rules of propriety, they will have a sense of shame, and moreover will come to be good."

2. 4 The Master said, "At fifteen I set my heart on learning. At thirty I could stand firm. At fourty I had no doubts. At fifty I knew the Decree of Heaven. At sixty I was already obedient (to this decree). At seventy I could follow the desires of my mind without overstepping the bounderies (of what is right)."

2. 5 Meng Yi Zi① asked about filial piety. The Master said, "Never go against ritual."

As Fan Chi② was driving him, the Master told him, 'Meng asked me about filial piety and I said 'Never go against ritual.' " Fan Chi asked, "What did you mean?" The Master replied, "when one's parents are alive, serve them according to ritual; when they are dead, bury them according to ritual, and sacrifice to them according to ritual."

2. 6 Meng Wu Bo③ asked what filial piety was. The master said, "The children should not make their parents worry about them except when they are ill."

---

① A young grandee of Lu, whose father sent him to study with Confucius.

② A disciple of Confucius.

③ The son of Meng Yi Zi.

為你的疾病擔憂。”

2·7 子游問孝。子曰:“今之孝者,是謂能養。至於犬馬,皆能有養;不敬,何以别乎?”

【譯文】子游問什麼是孝。孔子説:“現在的所謂‘孝’,只是説能夠養活父母就行了。連狗和馬都能夠得到飼養,如果對父母不恭敬,供養父母和飼養狗馬有什麼區别呢?”

2·8 子夏問孝。子曰:“色難。有事,弟子服其勞;有酒食,先生饌,曾是以爲孝乎?”

【譯文】子夏詢問什麼是孝。孔子説:“難在對父母和顏悦色。有事情,年輕人替他操勞;有酒飯,給父兄吃,難道這樣就算是孝了嗎?”

2·9 子曰:“吾與回言終日,不違,如愚。退而省其私,亦足以發,回也不愚。”

【譯文】孔子説:“我與顏回講話,他整天都不提出任何不同意見,像是愚笨。等他回去自己研究,也能有所發揮,顏回并不愚笨。”

2·10 子曰:“視其所以,觀其所由,察其所安,人焉廋哉?人焉廋哉?”

【譯文】孔子説:“看他所作所為,觀察他走過的道路,了解他安於什麼,那麼,這個人怎麼隱蔽得了呢?怎麼隱蔽得了呢?”

2·11 子曰:“溫故而知新,可以爲師矣。”

【譯文】孔子説:“溫習舊的知識,而能有新的體會,便可以做老師了。”

2. 7 Ziyou[1] asked what filial piety was. The Master said, "Filial piety nowdays means merely to support one's parents. But even dogs and horses can be cared for to that extent. Without the feeling of respect, wherein lies the difference?"

2. 8 Zixia asked what filial piety was. The Master said, "The difficulty is with a cheerful countenance all the time. If, when their parents have anything to be done, the children undertake the hard work, and if, when the children have wine and food, they serve their parents first, can this be called filial piety?"

2. 9 The Master said, "I can talk with Hui[2] for a whole day without his ever differing from me. He seems to be stupid. But when he is not with me I examine his conduct and find he is able to illustrate my teachings. He is by no means stupid."

2. 10 The Master said, "See what a man does, observe the roads he has followed, examine in what things he rests, how can a man conceal his real self? How can a man conceal his real self?"

2. 11 The Master said, "If a man can continually acquire new knowledge when he thinks over the old, he may be a teacher of others."

---

① A disciple of Confucius.

② i. e. Yan Yuan, disciple of Confucius.

2·12　子曰:"君子不器。"

【譯文】孔子說:"君子不像器皿一樣,只有一種用處。"

2·13　子貢問君子。子曰:"先行其言而後從之。"

【譯文】子貢問怎樣才能做一個君子。孔子說:"先把他心裏的話實行了,再說出來。"

2·14　子曰:"君子周而不比,小人比而不周。"

【譯文】孔子說:"君子團結而不互相勾結,小人互相勾結而不團結。"

2·15　子曰:"學而不思則罔,思而不學則殆。"

【譯文】孔子說:"讀書而不思考,就會迷惘;只是思考而不去讀書,就會感到疑惑。"

2·16　子曰:"攻乎異端,斯害也已。"

【譯文】孔子說:"批判不正確的議論,禍害就可以消除了。"

2·17　子曰:"由,誨女知之乎!知之爲知之,不知爲不知,是知也。"

【譯文】孔子說:"仲由,教給你什麼是智慧吧!知道的就說知道,不知道的就說不知道,這就是智慧。"

2·18　子張學干祿。子曰:"多聞闕疑,愼言其餘,則寡尤;多見闕殆,愼行其餘,則寡悔。言寡尤,行寡悔,祿在其中矣。"

【譯文】子張向孔子請教獲得官職和俸祿的方法。孔子說:"多聽些,有懷疑的地方,加以保留。其餘有把握的部份,謹愼地說出來,就能減少錯誤。多看些,有懷疑的地方,加以保留。其餘

2. 12 The Master said, "The superior man is not like a utensil, which only has one specific usage."

2. 13 Zigong asked how to be a superior man. The Master said, "He acts before he speaks, and afterwards speaks according to his actions."

2. 14 The Master said, "The superior man is broad-minded and not a partisan. The small man is a partisan and not broad-minded."

2. 15 The Master said, "He who learns without thinking is lost. He who thinks without learning remains puzzled."

2. 16 The Master said, "Criticizing those incorrect ideas may eliminate harm."

2. 17 The Master said, "You[①], I shall teach you what wisdom is. When you know a thing, say that you know it; when you do not know a thing, admit that you do not know it. This is wisdom."

2. 18 Zizhang[②] was learning to seek official post and salary. The Master said, "Hear much, remain silent to whatever you stand in doubt, and speak cautiously of the rest, then you will seldom fall into error. See much, put aside what you are doubtful about, and put the rest cautiously into practice,

---

① i. e. Zilu, disciple of Confucius.

② A disciple of Confucius.

有把握的部份，謹慎地去實行，就可以少後悔。言語錯誤少，行為后悔少，俸祿就在其中了。”

2·19 哀公問曰：“何爲則民服？”孔子對曰：“舉直錯諸枉，則民服；舉枉錯諸直，則民不服。”

【譯文】魯哀公問道：“怎樣做才能使百姓順服呢？”孔子回答說：“把正直的人提拔起來，安排在邪惡的人之上，百姓就順服了；若是把邪惡的人提拔起來，安排在正直的人之上，百姓就不會順服。”

2·20 季康子問：“使民敬、忠以勸，如之何？”子曰：“臨之以莊，則敬；孝慈，則忠；舉善而教不能，則勸。”

【譯文】 季康子問道：“要使百姓嚴肅認真、盡心竭力和互相勸勉，應該怎麼辦呢？”孔子說：“你對待百姓的事情嚴肅認真，百姓對待你也會嚴肅認真；你孝順父母，慈愛幼小，百姓對你也會盡心竭力；你提拔好人，教育能力弱的人，百姓也會互相勸勉。”

2·21 或謂孔子曰：“子奚不爲政？”子曰：“《書》云：‘孝乎惟孝，友于兄弟，施於有政。’是亦爲政，奚其爲爲政？”

【譯文】 有人對孔子說：“您為什麼不從政？”孔子說：“《尚書》上說：‘孝啊，只有孝順父母，友愛兄弟，把這種風氣推廣到政治方面。’這就是參與政治了，為什麼一定要做官才叫做參與政治呢？”

2·22 子曰：“人而無信，不知其可也。大車無輗，小車無軏，其何以行之哉？”

【譯文】 孔子說：“一個人不講信用，是不可以的。大車子

then you will seldom fall into repentance. If you seldom fall into error in your speech, and seldom fall into repentance in your conduct, you are likely to achieve official post and salary."

2.19 The Duke Ai [1] asked, "What should I do to make the people submit?" The Master replied, "Promote the upright and set them on top of the crooked, then the people will submit. Promote the crooked and set them on top of the upright, then the people will not submit."

2.20 Ji Kang Zi [2] asked how to cause the people to be respectful and loyal, and to urge themselves to virtue. The Master said, "Treat them with dignity, then they will respect you. show piety to your parents and kindness to your children, then they will be loyal to you. Promote the good and teach the incompetent, then they will seek to be virtuous."

2.21 Someone said to Confucius, "Why are you not engaged in the government?" The Master said, "The Book of History says, 'Filial piety! Be filial to your parents and kind to your brothers. These qualities are displayed in government.' This also is to engage in government. Why is it that only holding office can be said to be in government?"

2.22 The Master said, "I do not know how a man without truthfulness is to get on. It is like a large carriage without the cross bar and a small carriage without the collar-bar. How

---

① Duke of Lu from 494—468, B.C.

② A grandee of Lu.

没有固定横木的插銷，小車子没有固定横木的插銷，靠什麽來行進呢？”

2·23 子張問：“十世可知也？”子曰：“殷因於夏禮，所損益，可知也；周因於殷禮，所損益，可知也。其或繼周者，雖百世，可知也。”

【譯文】子張問：“今後十代禮儀制度的變革，可以預料嗎？”孔子説：“殷朝沿襲夏朝的禮儀制度，所廢除的和增益的，是能夠知道的；周朝沿襲殷朝的禮儀制度，所廢除的和增益的，也是能夠知道的。假如有人繼承了周朝，就是一百代以後，禮儀制度也是可以預料的。”

2·24 子曰：“非其鬼而祭之，諂也。見義不爲，無勇也。”

【譯文】孔子説：“不是自己祖先的神靈，卻去祭祀，這是獻媚。看見應該做的事情而不去做，這是没有勇氣。”

八佾篇第三

3·1 孔子謂季氏，“八佾舞於庭，是可忍也，孰不可忍也？”

【譯文】孔子談到季氏，説：“他用六十四人在庭院奏樂舞蹈，（這是天子用的禮樂，）這種事情都忍心幹得出來，還有什麽事情不可以忍心幹得出來呢？”

3·2 三家者以《雍》徹。子曰：“‘相維辟公，天子穆穆’，奚取於三家之堂？”

【譯文】仲孫、叔孫、季孫三家唱着《雍》詩來撤除祭祖的祭品。（這是天子使用的禮儀。）孔子説：“《雍》説：‘助祭的是諸侯，主祭的天子嚴肅静穆。’在三家祭祖的廟堂上，採取《雍》詩的哪

can they be made to go without them?"

2. 23 Zizhang asked whether the ritual ten generations hence could be foretold. Confucius said, "The Yin dynasty followed the system of rituals of the Xia dynasty: what is abandoned or added may be known. The Zhou dynasty followed the system of rituals of the Yin dynasty: what it abandoned or added may be known. If there is one that follows the Zhou dynasty, even one hundred generations hence, we can foretell its system of rituals."

2. 24 The Master said, "It is flattery for a man to sacrifice to a spirit which does not belong to him. It is cowardice to see what is right and not to do it."

BOOK Ⅲ BA YI

3. 1 The Master talked about the Head of the Ji family①, who had eight rows of eight dancers and singers each② performing in his courtyard, "If he can endure to do this, what else may he not endure to do?"

3. 2 The three families③ used the Yong Ode④ during the removal of the sacrificial vessels. The Master said, " 'Assisting are the princes; the son of Heaven looks profound and grave.' What possible application can such words in the Yong Ode

---

① One of the Three Families that had usurped most of the powers of the Duke of Lu.

② An imperial prerogative.

③ i. e. the families of Meng Sun, Shu Sun and Ji Sun.

④ An imperial prerogative.

一點意思呢？”

3·3 子曰：“人而不仁，如禮何？人而不仁，如樂何？”

【譯文】孔子說：“一個人，沒有仁德，怎樣對待禮儀制度呢？一個人，沒有仁德，怎樣對待音樂呢？”

3·4 林放問禮之本。子曰：“大哉問！禮，與其奢也，寧儉；喪，與其易也，寧戚。”

【譯文】林放詢問禮的根本。孔子說：“你問的真重要啊！就一般的禮儀說，與其奢侈浪費，寧可樸素節約；就喪禮說，與其儀式周到，寧可哀傷悲慟。”

3·5 子曰：“夷狄之有君，不如諸夏之亡也。”

【譯文】孔子說：“夷狄有君主，（卻沒有禮儀，）還不如中國沒有君主。（雖然沒有君主，卻有禮儀。）”

3·6 季氏旅於泰山。子謂冉有曰：“女弗能救與？”對曰：“不能。”子曰：“嗚呼！曾謂泰山不如林放乎？”

【譯文】季氏要去祭祀泰山。孔子對冉有說：“你不能阻止嗎？”冉有回答說：“不能。”孔子說：“哎呀！難道可以說泰山之神還不如林放懂得禮嗎？”

3·7 子曰：“君子無所爭。必也射乎！揖讓而升，下而飲。其爭也君子。”

【譯文】孔子說：“君子沒有什麼與人相爭的事情。（如果有所爭，）一定是比箭吧！（射箭時，）互相作揖，然後升堂。（射箭完畢，）走下堂來，互相敬酒。那種競爭是有禮貌的君子之爭。”

have in the hall of the three families?"

3.3 The Master said, "A man without human-heartedness, what has he to do with ritual? A man without human-heartedness, what has he to do with music?"

3.4 Lin Fang[1] asked for the main principles in connection with ritual. The Master said, "An important question indeed! In ritual at large, it is better to be sparing than lavish. In the mourning-rites, it is better to exhibit deep sorrow than to pay minute attention to observances."

3.5 The Master said, "The backward races, which even have their princes, are not as good as China which are without them."

3.6 The head of the Ji family was going to sacrifice to Mount Tai[2]. The Master said to Ran You[3], "Cannot you prevent him from doing this?" Ran You answered, "No, I cannot." The Master said, "Alas! Will you say that the spirit of Mount Tai knows less of ritual than Lin Fang?"

3.7 The Master said, "The superior man has no competition. If he has, he must have it in archery. But even then he bows (to his competitor) and thus goes up to the archery-ground. (After the competition), he descends and drinks with his competitor. In his competition, he is still a superior man."

---

① A person of Lu.

② To the spirit of Mount Tai, the prince alone had the right to sacrifice.

③ i. e. Ran Qiu, disciple of Confucius, who was in the service of the Ji family.

3·8 子夏問曰:"'巧笑倩兮,美目盼兮,素以爲絢兮。'何謂也?"子曰:"繪事後素。"

曰:"禮後乎?"子曰:"起予者商也!始可與言《詩》已矣。"

【譯文】子夏問道:"'笑容是多麼美好啊,眼睛是多麼動人啊,用素粉來打扮啊。'這幾句詩是什麼意思?"孔子説:"先有白色底子,然後才畫花。"

子夏説:"禮儀産生在仁義以后嗎?"孔子説:"啟發我的是卜商啊!現在可以和你討論《詩經》了。"

3·9 子曰:"夏禮,吾能言之,杞不足徵也;殷禮,吾能言之,宋不足徵也。文獻不足故也。足,則吾能徵之矣。"

【譯文】孔子説:"夏代的禮,我能説出來,(可是它的後世)杞國不足以作為證據;殷代的禮,我能説出來,(可是它的後世)宋國不足以作為證據。原因在於缺乏歷史文件和賢人。如果典籍充足,賢人衆多,我就可引以為證了。"

3·10 子曰:"禘自既灌而往者,吾不欲觀之矣。"

【譯文】孔子説:"(魯國舉行天子才能使用的)合祭祖先的盛大祭禮,從第一次獻酒以後,我就不想再看了。"

3·11 或問禘之説。子曰:"不知也。知其説者之於天下也,其如示諸斯乎!"指其掌。

【譯文】有人詢問大祭的禘禮。孔子説:"我不知道。知道的人對于治理天下,好像把東西擺在這裏一樣容易吧!"一面説,一面指着他的手掌。

3·12 祭如在,祭神如神在。子曰:"吾不與祭,如不祭。"

【譯文】孔子祭祀祖先的時候,好像祖先真在那裏。祭神的時

3.8 Zixia asked, "What is the meaning of the saying, 'How lovely is her artful smile! Her pretty eyes so black and white! The plain ground for the colours?'" The Master said, "The painting comes after the plain groundwork."

Zixia said, "Ritual then comes after human-heartedness and righteousness?" The Master said, "Shang①, it is you who can bring out my meaning! Now I can begin to talk about the Book of Poetry with you."

3.9 The Master said, "I am able to talk about the ritual of the Xia dynasty, but the state of Qi② cannot bear sufficient witness. I am able to talk about the ritual of the Yin dynasty, but the state of Song③ cannot bear sufficient witness. This is because of the lack both of their records and virtuous men. If those are sufficient I can adduce them to prove it."

3.10 The Master said, "At the great sacrifice, even after the libations have been poured, I have no wish to look on."

3.11 Someone asked for the meaning of the great sacrificial service. The Master said, "I do not know. He who knew the meaning would find it as easy to govern the empire as to lay things here." With these words, he pointed to his palm.

3.12 Confucius sacrified to the ancestors, as if they were present. He sacrified to the spirits, as if the spirits were pre-

---

① Zixia's personal name.

② The people of Qi are descendants of the Xia.

③ The people of Song are descendants of the Yin

候，好像神真在那裏。孔子說："我若是不參加祭祀，（讓人代祭，）就好像沒祭一樣。"

3·13 王孫賈問曰："'與其媚於奧，寧媚於竈'，何謂也？"子曰："不然獲罪於天，無所禱也。"

【譯文】王孫賈問道："'與其巴結住室西南角的奧神，還不如巴結竈君司命。'這兩句話是什麽意思？"孔子說："不對。如果得罪了上天，也就不用祈禱了。"

3·14 子曰："周監於二代，郁郁乎文哉！吾從周。"

【譯文】孔子說："周朝的禮樂制度借鑒於夏、商兩代，它多麽豐富多彩呀！我贊成周朝的禮樂。"

3·15 子入太廟，每事問。或曰："孰謂鄹人之子知禮乎？入太廟，每事問。"子聞之，曰："是禮也。"

【譯文】孔子到了周公廟，每件事情都詢問。有人說："誰說大夫的兒子懂得禮啊？到了周公廟，每件事都要詢問。"孔子聽到了這話，就說："這正是禮呀。"

3·16 子曰："射不主皮，爲力不同科，古之道也。"

【譯文】孔子說："（演習禮樂時，）射箭不一定要射穿箭靶子，因爲各人的氣力不一樣，這是古代的規矩。"

3·17 子貢欲去告朔之餼羊。子曰："賜也！爾愛其羊，我愛其禮。"

【譯文】子貢打算不用魯國每月初一告祭祖廟的那隻活羊。孔子說："賜呀！你愛惜那隻羊，我愛惜那種禮。"

sent. The Master said, "If I am not present at the sacrifice, I do not think I sacrifice at all."

3. 13 Wangsun Jia① asked, "What is the meaning of the saying, 'It is better to pay court to the kitchen-god② than to the god in the south-west corner③?'" The Master said, "It is not true. He who offends against Heaven has none to whom he can pray."

3. 14 The Master said, "The rituals of the Zhou dynasty are inherited and developed from the two preceding dynasties Xia and Shang. How complete and elegant its rituals are! I follow upon Zhou."

3. 15 When the Master entered the Grand Temple, he asked about everything. Someone said, "Who will say that the son of the villager from Zou④ knows the rules of propriety? He has entered the Grand Temple and asks about everything." When the Master heard the remark he said, "This is a rule of propriety."

3. 16 The Master said, "In archery it is not piercing the target that counts, since men differ in strength. This is the old way."

3. 17 Zigong wanted to do away with the offering of a live sheep at the inauguration of each new moon. The Master said, "Ci! You grudge the sheep, I love the ceremony."

---

① Minister in the state of Wei.

②③ These two gods both are small gods. The god in the southwest corner is considered more important than the kitchen god, though he has no real power.

④ A village where Confucius' s father lived.

3·18 子曰："事君盡禮，人以爲諂也。"

【譯文】孔子說："服事君主盡到禮節，別人還以為他在獻媚討好。"

3·19 定公問："君使臣，臣事君，如之何？"孔子對曰："君使臣以禮，臣事君以忠。"

【譯文】魯定公問："君主使用臣子，臣子侍奉君主，應該怎樣做？"孔子回答說："君主應該依照禮使用臣子，臣子侍奉君主應該忠心耿耿。"

3·20 子曰："《關雎》，樂而不淫，哀而不傷。"

【譯文】孔子說："《關雎》這篇詩，快樂而不放蕩，悲哀而不過分傷感。"

3·21 哀公問社於宰我。宰我對曰："夏后氏以松，殷人以柏，周人以栗，曰，使民戰栗。"子聞之，曰："成事不說，遂事不諫，既往不咎。"

【譯文】魯哀公問宰我，做土地神牌位用什麼木料。宰我回答說："夏代用松木，殷代用柏木，周代用栗木，意思是說使百姓戰栗。"孔子聽到後說："已經完成的事不用解釋了，已經做過的事不用勸阻了，已經過去的事不用追究了。"

3·22 子曰："管仲之器小哉！"

或曰："管仲儉乎？"曰："管氏有三歸，官事不攝，焉得儉？"

"然則管仲知禮乎？"曰："邦君樹塞門，管氏亦樹塞門。邦君爲兩君之好，有反坫，管氏亦有反坫。管氏而知禮，孰不知禮？"

【譯文】孔子說："管仲的器量狹小得很呀！"

有人問："管仲節儉嗎？"孔子說："管仲收取大量的市租，手

3. 18 The Master said, "He who serves his prince with all due rules of propriety would be thought a flatterer."

3. 19 The Duke Ding① asked how a prince should employ his ministers, and how ministers should serve their prince. The Master replied, "A prince should employ his ministers according to the rules of propriety; ministers should serve their prince with loyalty."

3. 20 The Master said, "The poem Guanju is expressive of joy without being licentious, and of grief not carried to the point of self-injury."

3. 21 The Duke Ai asked Zai Wo② about the altars erected in honour of the God of Earth. Zai Wo replied, "The Xia sovereign used the pine tree; the men of the Yin used the cypress; and the men of the Zhou used the chestnut tree, meaning thereby to cause the people to be in fear and trembling③." When the Master heard it, he said, "Things that are finished with, it is needless to discuss; things that have already taken their course, it is needless to remonstrate about; things that are past, it is needless to blame."

3. 22 The Master said, "How narrow-minded Guan Zhong④ was!"

Someone said, "Was Guan Zhong frugal?" The Master said, "He collected a huge amount of taxes, and his officers performed no double duties. How can he be considered frugal?"

---

① Duke of Lu.

② A disciple of Confucius.

③ Pun on li a chestnut-tree and li 'to be in fear and trembling'.

④ Prime Minister of the state of Qi.

下的人員從不兼職，怎麼能說是節儉呢？”

“那么管仲懂得禮節嗎？”孔子說：“國君在門口設立一個阻隔內外視綫的照壁，管仲也設立一個照壁。國君為了自己與其他國君的友好，宴會時在堂上設置放空酒杯的反坫，管仲也設置有反坫。如果說管仲懂得禮節，誰還不懂得禮節呢？”

3·23 子語魯大師樂，曰：“樂其可知也：始作，翕如也；從之，純如也，皦如也，绎如也，以成。”

【譯文】孔子對魯國的樂官太師談論音樂說：“音樂是可以通曉的。開始演奏，翕翕地熱烈；繼續下去，和諧而清晰，樂音繹繹地不絕，直到完成。”

3·24 儀封人請見，曰：“君子之至於斯也，吾未嘗不得見也。”從者見之。出曰：“二三子何患於喪乎？天下之無道也久矣，天將以夫子爲木鐸。”

【譯文】儀地的邊防官請求會見孔子，說：“有道德學問的人到了這個地方，我從來没有不和他見面的。”孔子的隨行學生帶他去見孔子。出來後，（對孔子的學生們）說：“你們這些人為什麼擔心得不到官職呢？天下黑暗腐敗的日子太長久了，上天將要把他老人家做為人民的導師。”

3·25 子謂《韶》，“盡美矣，又盡善也。”謂《武》，“盡美矣，未盡善也。”

【譯文】孔子談論（舜時的樂曲）《韶》說：“美妙極了，又非常完善。”談論到（周武王時的樂曲）《武》說：“美妙極了，還不夠完善。”

3·26 子曰：“居上不寬，爲禮不敬，臨喪不哀，吾何以觀之

"Then ,did Guan Zhong know the rules of propriety?" The Master said, "The prince of a state had a screen to intercept the view at the gates. Guan Zhong had such a screen. The prince of a state had a stand for turned-down cups when meeting other princes. Guan Zhong also had such a stand. If Guan Zhong knows the rules of propriety, who does not know them?"

3. 23 When talking about music with the grand music-master of Lu, the Master said, "How to play music can be known. At first each part is in unison. As it proceeds, they should be in harmony, severally distinct and flowing without break, and thus on to the close. "

3. 24 The frontier guardian at Yi asked to be introduced to the Master, saying, "When a superior man has arrived here, I have never failed to see him. "The Master' s followers presented him. When he came out from the interview, he said, "Why are you distressed by your fall? The empire has long been without the Way. Heaven is going to use your master as the guide to the people. "

3. 25 The Master said of the Shao① that it was perfectly beautiful and also perfectly good. He said of the Wu② that it was perfectly beautiful but not perfectly good.

3. 26 The Master said, "High officers without magna-

---

① The music mined the peaceful accession of the legendary Emperor Shun.

② The music mined the accession by conquest of the Emperor Wu, who overthrew the Yin dynasty.

哉!”

【譯文】孔子說:“處在上層地位不寬宏大量,舉行禮儀的時候不恭敬嚴肅,參加喪事的時候不悲哀,這我怎麼能看得下去呢!”

里仁篇第四

4·1 子曰:“里仁爲美。擇不處仁,焉得知?”

【譯文】孔子說:“住的地方要有仁德才好。如果選擇的住處沒有仁德,怎麼能算是聰明呢?”

4·2 子曰:“不仁者不可以久處約,不可以長處樂。仁者安仁,知者利仁。”

【譯文】孔子說:“不仁德的人不可能長久地處於窮困,也不可能長久地處於安樂。有仁德的人安心實行仁,聰明人知道仁合乎他的利益而實行仁。”

4·3 子曰:“唯仁者能好人,能惡人。”

【譯文】孔子說:“只有仁人才能夠(合理地)愛人和恨人。”

4·4 子曰:“苟志於仁矣,無惡也。”

【譯文】孔子說:“假如立定志向去實行仁德,也就不會做壞事。”

4·5 子曰:“富與貴,是人之所欲也;不以其道得之,不處也。貧與賤,是人之所惡也;不以其道得之,不去也。君子去仁,惡乎成名?君子無終食之間違仁,造次必於是,顛沛必於是。”

【譯文】孔子說:“發財和作官,是人人所盼望的;不用正當的

nimity; ceremonies performed without reverence; mourning conducted without grief---how can I bear to see such things?"

BOOK IV LI REN

4. 1 The Master said, "It is human-heartedness that constitutes the excellence of a neighborhood. How can a man be considered wise if, when he selects a residence, he does not fit on one where human-heartedness prevails?"

4. 2 The Master said, "Those who are without virtue cannot for long endure poverty and hardship, nor can they for long abide prosperity and enjoyment. The virtuous rest in virtue, whereas the wise pursue virtue in the belief that it pays to do so."

4. 3 The Master said, "Only those with perfect virtue can love and hate people."

4. 4 The Master said, "If a man sets his heart on virtue, he will practice nothing evil."

4. 5 The Master said, "Wealth and rank are what everyone desires; but if they cannot be obtained in proper way, a superior man will not accept them. Poverty and meanness are what everyone dislikes; but if they cannot be avoided in the

方法去得到它,就不去接受。窮困和下賤,是人人所厭惡的;不用正當的方法去擺脱它,就不擺脱。君子拋棄了仁德,怎樣去成就他的聲名呢?君子沒有一頓飯的時間離開仁德,在倉卒匆忙的時候一定這樣,在顛沛流離的時候也一定這樣。"

4·6 子曰:"我未見好仁者,惡不仁者。好仁者,無以尚之;惡不仁者,其爲仁矣,不使不仁者加乎其身。有能一日用其力於仁矣乎?我未見力不足者。蓋有之矣,我未之見也。"

【譯文】孔子説:"我沒有見到過喜愛仁德的人和厭惡不仁德的人。喜愛仁德的人,是再好不過了;厭惡不仁德的人,他實行仁德,只是不使不仁德的東西加到自己身上。有沒有人能夠一天把他的力量用在仁德上呢?我沒有見過力量不夠的。大概還是有的,只是我沒有見到。"

4·7 子曰:"人之過也,各於其黨。觀過,斯知仁矣。"

【譯文】孔子説:"人的錯誤,總是與和他同類的人相同的。考察所犯的錯誤,就可以知道他是什麼樣的人了。"

4·8 子曰:"朝聞道,夕死可矣。"

【譯文】孔子説:"早晨聽到真理,晚上死去都可以。"

4·9 子曰:"士志於道,而恥惡衣惡食者,未足與議也。"

【譯文】孔子説:"讀書人有志於真理,卻以穿得不好、吃得不好為恥辱,這種人便值不得同他談論了。"

4·10 子曰:"君子之於天下也,無適也,無莫也,義之與比。"

【譯文】孔子説:"君子對於天下的事情,沒有一定要怎樣

proper way, a superior man will not forsake them. If a superior man abandons virtue, how can he fulfil that name? Even for the space of a single meal the superior man does not go against virtue. In moments of haste, he cleaves to it. In seasons of danger, he cleaves to it."

4.6 The Master said, "I have never yet seen one who loved virtue, nor one who hated what was not virtuous. He who loved virtue would esteem nothing above it. He who hated what was not virtuous would practise virtue in such a way that what was not virtuous never had a chance to get at him. Is anyone able to apply all his strength to practising virtue for a whole day? I have not seen anyone whose strength is insufficient. There may possibly be such a man, but I have never seen one."

4.7 The Master said, "Men's faults are characteristic of the class to which they belong. By observing a man's faults, it may be known what kind of person he is."

4.8 The Master said, "To hear the Way in the morning and then die at night, that would be all right."

4.9 The Master said, "A scholar whose heart is set on the truth, but who is still ashamed of poor clothes and bad food, is not worth discussing truth with."

4.10 The Master said, "The superior man, in dealing with the world, does not set his mind either for anything, or against anything; what is right he will follow."

幹的模式，也沒有一定不要怎樣幹的模式，怎樣幹合情合理就怎樣幹。”

4·11 子曰:“君子懷德,小人懷土;君子懷刑,小人懷惠。”

【譯文】孔子說:“君子念念不忘道德,小人念念不忘田土;君子關心法度,小人關心個人好處。”

4·12 子曰:“放於利而行,多怨。”

【譯文】孔子說:“根據個人利益而行動,會招致很多的怨恨。”

4·13 子曰:“能以禮讓爲國乎?何有?不能以禮讓爲國,如禮何?”

【譯文】孔子說:“能夠用禮讓來治理國家嗎?這有什麽困難呢?如果不能用禮讓來治理國家,又怎樣來對待禮儀呢?”

4·14 子曰:“不患無位,患所以立。不患莫己知,求爲可知也。”

【譯文】孔子說:“不愁没有職位,只愁没有自立的本領;不怕没有人瞭解自己,但求有被別人瞭解的才能。”

4·15 子曰:“參乎!吾道一以貫之。”曾子曰:“唯。”

子出,門人問曰:“何謂也?”曾子曰:“夫子之道,忠恕而已矣。”

【譯文】孔子說:“參呀!我的學説貫穿着一個基本觀念。”曾子說:“是的。”

孔子走出去以後,別的學生問曾子說:“這是什麽意思?”曾子說:“他老人家的學説,只是忠和恕罷了。”

4. 11 The Master said, "The superior man thinks of virtue; the small man thinks of soil. The superior man thinks of laws, the small man thinks of favours which he may receive."

4. 12 The Master said, "He who acts solely for his own advantage will arouse much discontent."

4. 13 The Master said, "If a prince is able to govern his kingdom by the rules of propriety, what difficulty will he have? If he cannot do so, what has he to do with the rules of propriety?"

4. 14 The Master said, "I am not concerned that I am not in office. What I am concerned is how I may qualify myself for office. I am not concerned that I am not known. I seek to be worthy to be known."

4. 15 The Master said, "Shen[①]! All my teachings are linked together by one principle." "Quite so," replied Zeng Zi.

When the Master had left the room, the disciples asked, "What did he mean?" Zeng Zi replied, "Our Master's teaching consists of the principle of loyalty (Zhong) and consideration (Shun), and that is all."

---

① Personal name of Zeng Zi.

4·16 子曰:"君子喻於義,小人喻於利。"

【譯文】孔子說:"君子懂得義,小人懂得利。"

4·17 子曰:"見賢思齊焉,見不賢而內自省也。"

【譯文】孔子說:"看見賢人,便應該想向他看齊;看見不賢的人,便應該自我反省有沒有同他類似的毛病。"

4·18 子曰:"事父母幾諫,見志不從,又敬不違,勞而不怨。"

【譯文】孔子說:"侍奉父母,如果他們有不對的地方,應該婉轉地勸止。他們不聽從,仍然恭敬,不加違抗,雖然憂愁,但不怨恨。"

4·19 子曰:"父母在,不遠遊,遊必有方。"

【譯文】孔子說:"父母在世,不出遠門。如果要出遠門,必須有一定的去處。"

4·20 子曰:"三年無改於父之道,可謂孝矣。"

【譯文】孔子說:"父親死後,如果三年不改變父親之所為,可以說是盡孝了。"

4·21 子曰:"父母之年,不可不知也。一則以喜,一則以懼。"

【譯文】孔子說:"父母的年齡不能不知道,一方面因為他們高壽而高興,另一方面又為他們壽高而有所恐懼。"

4·22 子曰:"古者言之不出,恥躬之不逮也。"

4.16 The Master said, "The superior man comprehends righteousness (Yi); the small man comprehends profit (Li)."

4.17 The Master said, "When we see a man of virtue and talent, we should think of equalling them; when we see a man of a contrary character, we should turn inwards and examine ourselves."

4.18 The Master said, "In serving his parents, a son may gently remonstrate with them when they are wrong. But if he sees that they are not inclined to follow his advice, he should resume an attitude of reverence and not offend them; he may feel worried, but not resentful."

4.19 The Master said, "While his parents are alive, the son should not be far away from home. Or if he does so, he must have a fixed place to which he goes."

4.20 The Master said, "If the son for three years does not alter from the way of his father, he may be called filial."

4.21 The Master said, "The age of parents should always be kept in the memory, at once for joy and for fear."

4.22 The Master said, "The ancients did not readily give

【譯文】孔子說:“古時候人們不輕易把話說出口,因為他們以說得出而做不到為可恥。”

4·23 子曰:“以約失之者鮮矣。”

【譯文】孔子說:“因為對自己節制、約束而發生過失,這種情況是很少的。”

4·24 子曰:“君子欲訥於言而敏於行。”

【譯文】孔子說:“君子言語要遲鈍,行動要敏捷。”

4·25 子曰:“德不孤,必有鄰。”

【譯文】孔子說:“有道德的人不會孤單,一定會有人和他做伴。”

4·26 子游曰:“事君數,斯辱矣;朋友數,斯疏矣。”

【譯文】子游說:“侍奉君主過於煩瑣,就會招致侮辱;對待朋友過於親密,就會反被疏遠。”

公冶長篇第五

5·1 子謂公冶長,“可妻也。雖在縲絏之中,非其罪也。”以其子妻之。

【譯文】孔子談論公冶長,說“可以把女兒嫁給他。他雖然曾被關在監獄中,但不是他的罪過。”便把自己的女兒嫁給他。

5·2 子謂南容,“邦有道,不廢;邦無道,免於刑戮。”以其兄之子妻之。

【譯文】孔子談論南容,說他“國家政治清明時,總有官做,不

utterance to their words. Because they would feel disgraceful if their actions did not come up to them."

4.23 The Master said, "Those who err on the side of strictness are few indeed!"

4.24 The Master said, "The superior man should be slow in words and earnest in deeds."

4.25 The Master said, "A man of virtue will never be left to stand alone, he must have companions."

4.26 Zigong said, "In serving a prince, frequent remonstrances lead to disgrace. Between friends, frequent reproofs lead to estrangement."

BOOK V GONG YE CHANG

5.1 The Master said of Gongye Chang[①], "I may marry my daughter to this man. Although he has been put in prison, he was not guilty of any crime." He married his daughter to him.

5.2 The Master said of Nan Rong[②], "When the country was well governed, he would not be out of office; and when the

---

① A disciple of Confucius.

② A disciple of Confucius.

被廢棄;國家政治黑暗,也不致遭受刑罰。”於是把自己哥哥的女兒嫁給他。

5·3 子謂子賤,“君子哉若人!魯無君子者,斯焉取斯?”

【譯文】孔子評論宓子賤,說“這人是君子呀!假若魯國沒有君子,這種人從哪裏得到這種好品德呢?”

5·4 子貢問曰:“賜也何如?”子曰:“女,器也。”曰:“何器也?”曰:“瑚璉也。”

【譯文】子貢問道:“我是一個怎樣的人?”孔子說:“你好比是一個器皿。”子貢道:“什麼器皿?”孔子道:“宗廟裏盛黍稷的瑚璉。”

5·5 或曰:“雍也仁而不佞。”子曰:“焉用佞?禦人以口給,屢憎於人。不知其仁,焉用佞?”

【譯文】有人說:“冉雍這個人有仁德,卻沒有口才。”孔子說:“何必要口才呢?強嘴利舌地同人家辯駁,常常被人討厭。我不知道冉雍是否仁德,但為什麼要有口才呢?”

5·6 子使漆彫開仕。對曰:“吾斯之未能信。”子說。

【譯文】孔子叫漆彫開去作官。他回答說:“我對這個還沒有信心。”孔子很高興。

5·7 子曰:“道不行,乘桴浮于海。從我者,其由與?”子路聞之喜。子曰:“由也好勇過我,無所取材。”

【譯文】孔子說:“我的主張不能實行,只好坐着木筏到海外去,跟隨我的恐怕只有仲由吧?”子路聽到了很高興。孔子說:“仲由的勇敢精神超過了我,但不能裁奪事理。”

country was ill governed, he would avoid punishment." He married his elder brother's daughter to him.

5.3 The Master said of Zijian[1], "A superior man indeed is such a man! If there were no superior men in the state of Lu, how could he have acquired this virtue?"

5.4 Zigong asked, "What do you think of me?" The Master said, "You are a utensil." Zigong further asked, "What sort of utensil?" The Master said, "A fine sacrificial utensil."

5.5 Someone said, "Yong[2] is virtuous, but he is a poor talker." The Master said, "What is the good of being a good talker? Those who refute men with tongue-craft often bring about hatred to themselves. I do not know whether he is truely virtuous, but why must he be a good talker?"

5.6 The Master asked Qidiao Kai[3] to take office. He replied, "I do not have enough confidence for that yet." The Master was pleased.

5.7 The Master said, "If my doctrines make no way, I will get upon a raft and float out to sea. I am afraid only You would come with me." Zilu was glad to hear this. The Master said, "You is fonder of daring than I am. He does not exercise his judgement upon matters."

---

① A disciple of Confucius.

② i. e. Ran Yong, a disciple of Confucius.

③ A disciple of Confucius.

5·8 孟武伯問子路仁乎？子曰："不知也。"又問。子曰："由也，千乘之國，可使治其賦也，不知其仁也。"

"求也何如？"子曰："求也，千室之邑，百乘之家，可使爲之宰也，不知其仁也。"

"赤也何如？"子曰："赤也，束帶立於朝，可使與賓客言也，不知其仁也。"

【譯文】孟武伯向孔子問子路有沒有仁德。孔子說："不曉得。"他又問。孔子說："仲由這個人，如果有一千輛兵車的國家，可以叫他負責兵役和軍政的工作。至於他有沒有仁德，我卻不曉得。"

孟武伯繼續問："冉求這人又怎麽樣呢？"孔子道："求啊，千戶人口的縣，可以叫他當縣長；百輛兵車的大夫封地，可以叫他當總管。至於他有沒有仁德，我也不曉得。"

"公西赤又怎麽樣呢？"孔子說："赤啊，穿着禮服，立於朝廷之中，可以叫他接待外賓，辦理交涉。至於他有沒有仁德，我也不曉得。"

5·9 子謂子貢曰："女與回也孰愈？"對曰："賜也何敢望回？回也聞一以知十，賜也聞一以知二。"子曰："弗如也；吾與女弗如也。"

【譯文】孔子對子貢說："你和顏回，哪一個強些？"子貢回答說："我怎敢和回相比？回聽到一件事，可以推知十件事；我聽到一件事，只能推知兩件事。"孔子說："趕不上他；我同意你的話，是趕不上他。"

5·10 宰予晝寢。子曰："朽木不可雕也，糞土之牆不可杇也；於予與何誅？"子曰："始吾於人也，聽其言而信其行；今吾於

5.8 Meng Wu Bo asked whether Zilu was perfectly virtuous. The Master said, "I do not know. "He asked again, the Master replied, "In a country of a thousand chariots, You might be trusted to manage the military forces, but I do not know whether he is perfectly virtuous. "

"And what do you say of Qiu①?"The Master replied. "In a country of a thousand families, or in a house of a hundred chariots, Qiu might be trusted as governor, but I do not know whether he is perfectly virtuous. "

"What do you say of Chi②?"The Master replied, "In his full dress, standing in a court, Chi might well be charged to converse with the visitors and guests, but I do not know whether he is perfectly virtuous. "

5.9 The Master said to Zigong, "Who is the better, you or Hui?" Zigong replied, "How dare I compare myself with Hui? When hearing one thing, Hui is able to know ten other things; When hearing one thing I can only know two. "The Master said, "You are not equal to him. I agree with you. You are not equal to him. "

5.10 Zai Yu③ slept during the day time. The Master said, "Rotten wood cannot be carved, a wall of dried dung can-

---

① i. e. Ran You.

② i. e. Gongxi Hua, disciple of Confucius.

③ i. e. Zai Wo, disciple of Confucius.

人也，聽其言而觀其行。於予與改是。”

【譯文】宰予在白天睡覺。孔子說：“腐爛了的木頭不可雕刻，糞土似的牆壁粉刷不得；對於宰予不值得責備。”又說：“最初我對人家，聽到他的話，便相信他的行為；今天，我對人家，聽到他的話，卻要考察他的行為。從宰予的這件事以後，我改變了態度。”

5·11　子曰：“吾未見剛者。”或對曰：“申棖。”子曰：“棖也慾，焉得剛？”

【譯文】孔子說：“我沒見過剛毅不屈的人。”有人回答說：“申棖是這樣的人。”孔子說：“申棖慾望太多，哪裏能夠剛毅不屈？”

5·12　子貢曰：“我不欲人之加諸我也，吾亦欲無加諸人。”子曰：“賜也，非爾所及也。”

【譯文】子貢說：“我不想別人強加於我，我也不想強加於別人。”孔子說：“賜，這不是你所能做到的。”

5·13　子貢曰：“夫子之文章，可得而聞也；夫子之言性與天道，不可得而聞也。”

【譯文】子貢說：“老師關於文獻方面的學問，我們聽得到；老師關於天性和天道的言論，我們聽不到。”

5·14　子路有聞，未之能行，唯恐有聞。

【譯文】子路聽到某件事，還沒有能夠去做，便唯恐聽到另一件事。

5·15　子貢問曰：“孔文子何以謂之‘文’也？”子曰：“敏而

not be trowelled. This Yu! What is the use of my scolding him?" The Master went on to say, "Before, I merely listen to what people said and gave them credit for their conduct. Now I not only give ear to what they say, but also keep an eye on what they do, It was my dealings with Yu that brought about this change."

5. 11 The Master said, "I have never yet seen a steadfast man." Someone replied, "There is Shen Cheng!" The Master said, "Cheng, he has too many desires, how can he be called steadfast?"

5. 12 Zigong said, "What I do not want others to do to me, I also do not want to do to others." The Master said, "Ci, this is not what you can attain to."

5. 13 Zigong said, "The Master's teaching about historical records may be heard. But his discourses about man's nature and the way of Heaven cannot be heard."

5. 14 When Zilu heard anything, and had not yet put it into practice, he was only afraid that he would hear something else.

5. 15 Zigong asked, saying, "Why was Kong Wen Zi con-

好學,不恥下問,是以謂之'文'也。"

【譯文】子貢問道:"孔文子憑什麼謚號為'文'?"孔子說:"他聰敏好學,謙虛下問,不以為恥,所以用'文'字做他的謚號。"

5·16 子謂子産,"有君子之道四焉:其行己也恭,其事上也敬,其養民也惠,其使民也義。"

【譯文】孔子評論子産,說他"有四種行為合於君子之道:他自己的行為莊重,他奉事君主恭敬,他養護人民有恩惠,他役使人民合乎道理。"

5·17 子曰:"晏平仲善與人交,久而敬之。"

【譯文】孔子說:"晏平仲善於和別人交朋友,相交越久,越發恭敬別人。"

5·18 子曰:"臧文仲居蔡,山節藻梲,何如其知也?"

【譯文】孔子說:"臧文仲替一種叫蔡的大烏龜蓋了一間屋,有彫刻着像山一樣的斗栱和畫着藻草的梁上短柱,這個人的聰明怎麼會這樣呢?"

5·19 子張問曰:"令尹子文三仕爲令尹,無喜色;三已之,無慍色。舊令尹之政,必以告新令尹。何如?"子曰:"忠矣。"曰:"仁矣乎?"曰:"未知。焉得仁?"

"崔子弒齊君,陳文子有馬十乘,棄而違之。至於他邦,則曰,'猶吾大夫崔子也。'違之。之一邦,則又曰:'猶吾大夫崔子也。'違之。何如?"子曰:"清矣。"曰:"仁矣乎?"曰:"未知。焉得仁?"

【譯文】子張問道:"楚國的令尹子文三次做令尹的官,沒有高興的顏色;三次被罷免,沒有怨恨的顏色。自己任內的工作,一

ferred the posthumous title of Wen (cultured)?" The Master said, "He was diligent and fond of learning, and he was not ashamed to ask and learn from his inferiors. That is why he has been conferred the posthumous title of Wen."

5. 16 The Master said of Zichan[1], "He had four of the virtues of a superior man: in his own conduct, he was courteous; in serving his superiors, he was respectful; in nourishing the people, he was gracious; in ordering the people, he was just."

5. 17 The Master said, "Yan Ping Zhong[2] knew well how to make friends with others. The acquaintance might be long, he maintained the same respect to others."

5. 18 The Master said, "To keep a big tortoise, Zang Wen Zhong[3] built a hall with the hill-pattern on its pillar tops and the duckweed pattern on its beams[4]. Of what sort was his wisdom?"

5. 19 Zizhang asked, saying, "The minister Ziwen was three times appointed to that position, and manifested no joy in his countenance. Three times he was removed from office, and manifested no displeasure. Each time he made it a point to inform the new minister of the administration of state affairs during his tenure of office, What would you say of him?" The Master said, "He was loyal." "Was he perfectly virtuous?" "I

---

① Minister of the state of Zheng, died 522 B. C.

② Minister of the state of Qi, famous for his wise counsels, died in 500 B. C.

③ Minister of Lu in the seventy century B. C.

④ Such decoration was proper only to the Emperor's ancestral temple and palace.

定告訴下一屆的令尹。這個人怎麼樣?”孔子說:“可算盡忠於國家了。”子張說:“算不算仁呢?”孔子說:“不曉得。這怎麼能算是仁呢?”

子張又問:“崔杼殺掉齊莊公,陳文子有駕十輛車的四十匹馬,捨棄不要,離開齊國。到了另一個國家,說道:‘這裏的執政者同我們的崔子差不多。’又離開。又到了一國,又說道:‘這里的執政者同我們的崔子差不多。’於是又離開。這個人怎麼樣?”孔子說:“清白得很。”子張說:“算不算仁呢?”孔子說:“不曉得。這怎么能算是仁呢?”

5·20 季文子三思而後行。子聞之,曰:“再,斯可矣。”

【譯文】季文子每件事都考慮多次才去行動。孔子聽到了,說:“想兩次,也就可以了。”

5·21 子曰:“甯武子,邦有道,則知;邦無道,則愚。其知可及也,其愚不可及也。”

【譯文】孔子說:“甯武子在國家政治清明時便聰明;在國家政治黑暗時便裝傻。他那種聰明,別人趕得上;那種裝傻,別人就趕不上了。”

5·22 子在陳,曰:“歸與!歸與!吾黨之小子狂簡,斐然成章,不知所以裁之。”

【譯文】孔子在陳國,說:“回去吧!回去吧!家鄉的學生們有進取心、有大志,文彩也斐然可觀,但不知道怎樣節制自己。”

5·23 子曰:“伯夷、叔齊不念舊惡,怨是用希。”

【譯文】孔子說:“伯夷、叔齊這兩兄弟不記舊恨宿怨,別人對

do not know. How can he be called perfectly virtuous?"

Zizhang proceeded, "When the officer Cui Zi assassinated the sovereign of the State of Qi, Chen Wen Zi①, though he had forty horses, abandoned them and left the country. Coming to another state, he said, 'The officials here are no better than Cui Zi.' and left. Coming to the next state, he said, 'The officials here are no better than Cui Zi.' and left also. What would you say of him?" The Master said, "He was stainless." "Was he perfectly virtuous?" "I do not know. How can he be called perfectly virtuous?"

5.20 Ji Wen Zi② acted only after thinking thrice. When the Master heard of this, he said, "Twice may do."

5.21 The Master said, "When the right way prevailed in the country, Ning Wu Zi③ showed his wisdom. When the wrong way prevailed in the country, he showed his folly. Others may attain to his wisdom, but they cannot attain to his folly."

5.22 When the Master was in the state of Chen, he said, "Let me go back! Let me go back! My students at home are ambitious and they are literarily accomplished, but they do not know how to restrict and shape themselves."

5.23 The Master said, "Boyi and Shuqi④ did not keep the

---

① High official of Qi.

② High Official of Lu.

③ High Official of Wei.

④ Boyi and Shuqi were sons of the prince of Gu Zhu. Their father left the throne to the younger of the two; but he would not supplant the elder, nor would the elder act against his father's wishes. So they both retired into obscurity. When King Wu overthrew the tyrant Zhou, rather than live under a new dynasty, they starved to death.

他們的怨恨也就很少。”

5·24 子曰：“孰謂微生高直？或乞醯焉，乞諸其鄰而與之。”

【譯文】孔子說：“誰說微生高這個人直爽？有人向他討點醋，他到鄰居那裏要來送給那人。”

5·25 子曰：“巧言、令色、足恭，左丘明恥之，丘亦恥之。匿怨而友其人，左丘明恥之，丘亦恥之。”

【譯文】孔子說：“花言巧語，討好的臉色，十足的恭順，這種態度，左丘明認為可恥，我也認為可恥。內心藏着怨恨，表面上卻同他要好，這種行為，左丘明認為可恥，我也認為可恥。”

5·26 顏淵、季路侍。子曰：“盍各言爾志？”子路曰：“願車馬衣輕裘與朋友共敝之而無憾。”

顏淵曰：“願無伐善，無施勞。”

子路曰：“願聞子之志。”

子曰：“老者安之，朋友信之，少者懷之。”

【譯文】顏淵、季路陪侍着孔子。孔子說：“何不各人說說自己的志向？”

子路說：“願意把我的車馬、衣服、皮裘和朋友共同使用，壞了也沒有什麽不滿。”

顏淵說：“願意不誇耀自己的好處，不表白自己的功勞。”

子路向孔子說：“希望聽到您的志向。”

孔子說：“安慰老人，信任朋友，關懷青年。”

5·27 子曰：“已矣乎，吾未見能見其過而內自訟者也。”

【譯文】孔子說：“算了吧！我沒有看見過能夠看到自己的錯

wrongs done to them in mind, and hence few resentments directed towards them."

5.24 The Master said, "Who can say that Weisheng Gao is upright? Someone asked some vinegar of him, and he begged it from his neighbour and then gave it him (as from himself)."

5.25 The Master said, "Clever talk, flattering looks and overdone humility---Zuoqiu Ming was ashamed of them. I am also ashamed of them. To conceal resentment against a person and appear friendly with him---Zuoqiu Ming was ashamed of it. I am also ashamed of it."

5.26 Yan Hui and Jilu[①] were standing by his side; the Master said to them, "Why do not you each tell me your wishes?"

Zilu said, "I should like to share chariots and horses, clothes and fur with my friends, and if they wear them out, I would not be displeased."

Yan Hui said, "I should like not to boast of my good qualities, nor to display my meritorious deeds."

Zilu then said, "I should like to hear your wishes."

The Master said, "In dealing with the aged, to be of comfort to them; in dealing with friends, to show them sincerity; in dealing with the young, to cherish them."

5.27 The Master said, "Alas! I have never seen one who

---

① i.e. Zilu.

誤便在內心自我責備的。"

5·28 子曰:"十室之邑,必有忠信如丘者焉,不如丘之好學也。"

【譯文】孔子說:"十戶人家的地方,一定有像我這樣又忠心又信實的人,只是趕不上我愛好學習。"

雍也篇第六

6·1 子曰:"雍也可使南面。"

【譯文】孔子說:"冉雍這個人,可以讓他作長官。"

6·2 仲弓問子桑伯子。子曰:"可也簡。"仲弓曰:"居敬而行簡,以臨其民,不亦可乎?居簡而行簡,無乃大簡乎?"子曰:"雍之言然。"

【譯文】仲弓問及子桑伯子這個人。孔子說:"他簡單得好。"仲弓道:"若存心是嚴肅認真的,又執簡以馭繁來治理百姓,不也可以嗎?若存心是簡單的,又以簡單行之,不是太簡單了嗎?"孔子說:"你的話是正確的。"

6·3 哀公問:"弟子孰爲好學?"孔子對曰:"有顏回者好學,不遷怒,不貳過。不幸短命死矣,今也則亡,未聞好學者也。"

【譯文】魯哀公問:"你的學生中,哪個好學?"孔子回答說:"有一個叫顏回的人好學,不拿別人出氣,也不再犯同樣的過失。不幸短命死了,現在再沒有這樣的人了,再也沒聽到過好學的人了。"

6·4 子華使於齊,冉子爲其母請粟。子曰:"與之釜。"

could perceive his own faults and accuse himself inwardly."

5.28 The Master said, "In a hamlet of ten families, there may be found someone who is quite as loyal and sincere as I am, but not so fond of learning."

BOOK VI YONG YE

6.1 The Master said, "Yong[1], he can be made an official."

6.2 Zhonggong[2] asked about Zisang Bozi. The Master said, "He would do. He does not mind small matters."

Zhonggong said, "If a man cherishes a reverential feeling for business in himself, though he may be lax in small matters, his governing of the people may be approved. But if he cherishes that easy feeling in himself, and also carries it out in practice, is he not too lax?" The Master said, "What Yong says is right."

6.3 Duke Ai asked which of the disciples loved learning. The Master replied, "There was Hui. He loved learning. He did not vent his anger upon the innocent, nor did he repeat a fault. Unfortunately he was short-lived and died. Now there is no such a person. I have not yet heard of anyone who loves learning."

6.4 When Zihua[3] was sent on a mission to the state of

---

① i.e. Ran Yong.

② i.e. Ran Yong.

③ i.e. Gongxi Hua.

請益。曰:“與之庾。”

冉子與之粟五秉。

子曰:“赤之適齊也,乘肥馬,衣輕裘。吾聞之也:君子周急不繼富。”

【譯文】子華被派到齊國去作使者,冉有替他母親向孔子請求小米。孔子説:“給他六斗四升。”

冉有請求增加。孔子説:“再給他二斗四升。”

冉有卻給了他八十石。

孔子説:“公西赤到齊國去,坐着由肥馬駕的車輛,穿着又輕又暖的皮袍。我聽説過:君子雪裏送炭,不去錦上添花。”

6·5 原思爲之宰,與之粟九百,辭。子曰:“毋!以與爾鄰里鄉黨乎!”

【譯文】原思擔任孔子家的總管,孔子給他小米九百斗,他不肯接受。孔子説:“不要推辭!有多的就分給你當地的窮人吧!”

6·6 子謂仲弓,曰:“犂牛之子騂且角,雖欲勿用,山川其舍諸?”

【譯文】孔子談到冉雍,説:“耕牛生下的牛犢,長着赤色的毛,端正的角,雖然不想用它作為祭品,山川之神難道會捨棄它嗎?”

6·7 子曰:“回也,其心三月不違仁,其餘則日月至焉而已矣。”

【譯文】孔子説:“顔回,他的心長久地不離開仁德,别的學生只是短時期內做到仁罷了。”

6·8 季康子問:“仲由可使從政也與?”子曰:“由也果,於

Qi, the disciple Ran You asked for grain for Zihua's mother. The Master said, "Give her a Fu (equals **6.4** Chinese bushels).

Ran You requested more. The Master said, "Give her a Yu (equals **16** Chinese bushels)."

Ran You gave her five Bings (equals **800** Chinese bushels).

The Master said, "When Chi① went to Qi, he had sleek horses attached to his carriage, and wore light furs. I have heard that a superior man helps the needy but does not add to the wealth of the rich."

6.5 When Yuan Si② was made a governor of the Master's family, he was given an allowance of nine hundred measures of grain, but Yuan Si declined them. The Master said, "Do not decline them. May you not give them to your neighbors or villagers?"

6.6 The Master said of Zhonggong, "The calf of a brindled cow has red fur and fine horns. Although man may not want to use it in sacrifice, would the spirits of the mountains and rivers reject it?"

6.7 The Master said, "Hui is capable of occupying his whole mind for a long time with no thought but that of perfect virtue. Others can do so only in a short time."

6.8 Ji Kang Zi asked, "Is Zhong You③ fit to be employed

---

① i. e. Gongxi Hua.
② A disciple of Confucius.
③ i. e. Zilu.

從政乎何有？”

曰：“賜也可使從政也與？”曰：“賜也達，於從政乎何有？”

曰：“求也可使從政也與？”曰：“求也藝，於從政乎何有？”

【譯文】季康子問孔子：“仲由這人，可以使用他治理政事嗎？”孔子說：“仲由果敢決斷，讓他治理政事有什麼困難呢？”

又問：“端木賜可以使用他治理政事嗎？”孔子說：“端木賜通情達理，讓他治理政事有什麼困難呢？”

又問：“冉求可以使用他治理政事嗎？”孔子說：“冉求多才多藝，讓他治理政事有什麼困難呢？”

6·9 季氏使閔子騫爲費宰。閔子騫曰：“善爲我辭焉！如有復我者，則吾必在汶上矣。”

【譯文】季氏叫閔子騫作費邑的縣長。閔子騫對來人說：“好好地替我辭掉吧！若是再來找我的話，那我一定會逃到汶水之北去了。”

6·10 伯牛有疾，子問之，自牖執其手，曰：“亡之，命矣夫！斯人也而有斯疾也！斯人也而有斯疾也！”

【譯文】伯牛生了病，孔子去探問他，從窗戶裏握着他的手，說：“難得活了，這是命呀！這樣的人竟有這樣的病！這樣的人竟有這樣的病。”

6·11 子曰：“賢哉，回也！一簞食，一瓢飲，在陋巷，人不堪其憂，回也不改其樂。賢哉，回也！”

【譯文】孔子說：“顏回多麼賢明呀！一竹筐飯，一瓜瓢水，住在簡陋的巷子裏，別人都受不了那種窮苦，顏回卻不改變自己的樂趣。顏回多麼賢明呀！”

in the government?"The Master said,"Zhong You is a man of decision, what difficulty would he find in being a government official?"

Ji Kang Zi asked,"Is Ci fit to be employed in the government?"The Master said,"Ci is a man of intelligence, what difficulty would he find in being a government official?"

"Is Qiu fit to be employed in the government?"The Master said,"Qiu is a man of various ability, what difficulty would he find in being a government official?"

6.9 The Head of the Ji family sent to ask Min Ziqian①to be governor of Fei County. Min Ziqian said,"Decline the offer for me politely. If anyone comes again to invite me, I shall certainly be obliged to go to the far side of Wen River."

6.10 When Boniu②was ill, the Master went to ask after him. He took hold of his hand through the window, and said, "He is dying. It is fate, alas! ---Such a man had such a sickness! Such a man should had such a sickness!"

6.11 The Master said,"Virtuous indeed was Hui! With a single bamboo dish of rice, a single gourd of water, and living in a lowly lane, others could not endure such distress, but he did not allow it to affect his joy. Virtuous indeed was Hui!"

---

① A disciple of Confucius.

② A disciple of Confucius.

6·12　冉求曰:“非不説子之道,力不足也。”子曰:“力不足者,中道而廢。今女晝。”

【譯文】冉求説:“不是不喜歡您的學説,是我能力不夠。”孔子説:“如果能力不夠,是走到中途走不動了才停止。現在你是劃定了一個界限不肯起步。”

6·13　子謂子夏曰:“女爲君子儒,無爲小人儒。”

【譯文】孔子對子夏説:“你要做個君子式的儒者,不要去做那小人式的儒者。”

6·14　子游爲武城宰。子曰:“女得人焉耳乎?”曰:“有澹臺滅明者,行不由徑,非公事,未嘗至於偃之室也。”

【譯文】子游做武城縣長。孔子説:“你在這兒得到什麽人才了嗎?”他説:“有一個叫澹臺滅明的人,走路不走小道,不是公事,未曾到我屋裏來。”

6·15　子曰:“孟之反不伐,奔而殿,將入門,策其馬,曰:‘非敢後也,馬不進也。’”

【譯文】孔子説:“孟之反不誇耀自己,打敗仗逃跑時殿後掩護,將進城門,便鞭打着馬匹,説:‘不是我敢於殿後,是馬匹不肯快走。’”

6·16　子曰:“不有祝鮀之佞,而有宋朝之美,難乎免於今之世矣。”

【譯文】孔子説:“假使没有祝鮀的口才,卻有宋朝的美麗,在今天的社會裏恐怕難得避免禍害了。”

6·17　子曰:“誰能出不由户?何莫由斯道也?”

6. 12 Ran Qiu said, "It is not that I do not like your doctrines. It is just that I do not have enough strength." The Master said, "Those who do not have enough strength give up half way, but now you limit yourself and do not even desire to go."

6. 13 The Master said to Zixia, "You should be a scholar after the style of the superior man, and not after the style of the small man."

6. 14 When Ziyou was the governor of Wucheng, the Master said to him, "Have you got good men there?" He answered, "There is Dantai Mieming, who never takes a short cut in walking, and never comes to my house except on public business."

6. 15 The Master said, "Men Zhifan does not boast himself. He was the last in the flight from enemy. But when his men neared the city-gate, he whipped his horse saying, "It was not that I dared to be last. My horse would not gallop."

6. 16 The Master said, "If one only has the beauty of the prince Song Zhao but hasn' t the eloquence of Zhu Tuo, it will be difficult for him to avoid injury during these days."

6. 17 The Master said, "Who can go out of a house but by the door? How is it then that no one follow this Way?"

【譯文】孔子說:"誰能夠走出屋外不從房門經過,為什麼沒有人從這條路行走呢?"

6·18 子曰:"質勝文則野,文勝質則史。文質彬彬,然後君子。"

【譯文】孔子說:"樸實超過文采,就未免粗野;文采超過樸實,又未免虛浮。文采和樸實配合適當,這才是個君子。"

6·19 子曰:"人之生也直,罔之生也幸而免。"

【譯文】孔子說:"人的生存是靠正直,不正直的人也可以生存,那是他僥倖地免於禍害。"

6·20 子曰:"知之者不如好之者,好之者不如樂之者。"

【譯文】孔子說:"對於任何學問和事業,懂得它的人不如喜愛它的人,喜愛它的人又不如以它為樂的人。"

6·21 子曰:"中人以上,可以語上也;中人以下,不可以語上也。"

【譯文】孔子說:"中等水平以上的人,可以告訴他高深的道理;中等水平以下的人,不可以告訴他高深的道理。"

6·22 樊遲問知。子曰:"務民之義,敬鬼神而遠之,可謂知矣。"

問仁。曰:"仁者先難而後獲,可謂仁矣。"

【譯文】樊遲問怎麼樣才算聰明。孔子說:"致力於治理百姓所該做的,嚴肅地對待鬼神,卻遠離它,可以說是聰明了。"

又問怎麼樣才叫做有仁德。孔子說:"有仁德的人對艱難的工作搶先幹,對獲利的事情卻退居別人後面,這可算是仁德了。"

6. 18 The Master said, "Natural substance prevailing over ornamentation begets roughness; ornamentation prevailing over natural substance begets pedantry; natural substance and ornamentation duly blended make a superior man."

6. 19 The Master said, "Man's life depends on uprightness. He who goes on living without it escapes from death merely by good fortune."

6. 20 The Master said, "They who love it are better than those who know it, and they who delight in it are better than those who love it."

6. 21 The Master said, "To those who are above average, the high subjects may be discussed. To those who are below average, the high subjects may not be discussed."

6. 22 Fan Chi asked about wisdom. The Master said, "To devote oneself to the people's just cause, and, while respecting spiritual beings, to keep aloof from them, may be called wisdom." He asked about perfect virtue. The Master said, "The man of virtue vies for the hardest job and is the last for fame and gain; —this may be called perfect virtue."

6·23 子曰:"知者樂水,仁者樂山。知者動,仁者靜。知者樂,仁者壽。"

【譯文】孔子説:"聰明人樂於水,仁德的人樂於山。聰明人活躍,仁德的人沉靜。聰明人快樂,仁德的人長壽。"

6·24 子曰:"齊一變,至於魯;魯一變,至於道。"

【譯文】孔子説:"齊國改革,便達到魯國的水平;魯國一改革,便達到先王的大道了。"

6·25 子曰:"觚不觚,觚哉!觚哉!"

【譯文】孔子説:"觚不像個觚,這也是觚嗎!這也是觚嗎!"

6·26 宰我問曰:"仁者,雖告之曰,'井有仁焉',其從之也?"子曰:"何爲其然也?君子可逝也,不可陷也;可欺也,不可罔也。"

【譯文】宰我問道:"有仁德的人,就是告訴他説,'井裏掉下一位仁人',是不是就會跟着下去呢?"孔子説:"為什麼你要這樣做呢?你如果不喜歡君子,可以叫他遠遠走開不再回來,卻不可以陷害他;可以欺騙他,卻不可以愚弄他。"

6·27 子曰:"君子博學於文,約之以禮,亦可以弗畔矣夫!"

【譯文】孔子説:"君子廣泛地學習文獻,再用禮節來加以約束,也就可以不致於離經叛道了。"

6·28 子見南子,子路不説。夫子矢之曰:"予所否者,天厭之!天厭之!"

6. 23 The Master said, "The wise delight in water; the virtuous delight in mountains. The wise are active; the virtuous are tranquil. The wise are happy; the virtuous are long-lived."

6. 24 A single change could bring Qi to the level of Lu; and a single chang could bring Lu to the Way."

6. 25 The Master said, "A Gu[1] is not like a Gu. Is it a Gu? Is it a Gu?"

6. 26 Zai Wo asked, "A benevolent man, if he was told that there was another benevolent man in the well, will he go in after him?" The Master said, "Why should you do so? If you do not like the superior man, you may let him go away from you and never go back, but you cannot frame him. You may deceive him, but cannot fool him."

6. 27 The Master said, "The superior man, who is widely versed in historical records and keeps himself under the restraint of the rules of propriety, may thus not overstep what is right."

6. 28 The Master had visited Nan Zi[2]. Zilu was displeased at this. The Master swore, saying, "Wherein I have

---

① A kind of drinking vessal.

② The dissolute wife of Duke Ling of Wei.

【譯文】孔子去和南子相見，子路不高興。孔子發誓道："我假若不對的話，天厭棄我！天厭棄我！"

6·29　子曰："中庸之爲德也，其至矣乎！民鮮久矣。"

【譯文】孔子說："中庸這種道德，該是最高的了，大家已是長久地缺乏了。"

6·30　子貢曰："如有博施於民而能濟衆，何如？可謂仁乎？"子曰："何事於仁！必也聖乎！堯舜其猶病諸！夫仁者，己欲立而立人，己欲達而達人。能近取譬，可謂仁之方也已。"

【譯文】子貢說："假若有人廣泛地給人民好處，又能幫助大家生活得很好，怎麽樣？可以說是仁德了嗎？"孔子說："哪里只是有仁德！一定是聖德了！堯和舜或者都難以做到。仁是什麽呢？自己要站得住，便同時也使別人站得住；自己要事事行得通，同時也使別人事事行得通。能夠推己及人，可以說是實行仁德的方法了。"

述而篇第七

7·1　子曰："述而不作，信而好古，竊比於我老彭。"

【譯文】孔子說："傳述而不創作，相信并喜愛古代文化，我私自把自己和老彭相比。"

7·2　子曰："默而識之，學而不厭，誨人不倦，何有於我哉？"

【譯文】孔子說："把所見所聞默默地記在心裏，學習而不滿足，教導別人而不疲倦，這些事情我做到了哪些呢？"

done amiss, may Heaven reject me! May Heaven reject me!"

6.29 The Master said, "Perfect is the virtue Golden Mean! Among the people, it has long been rare."

6.30 Zigong asked, "Suppose there is a man who can extensively confer benefits on the people and assist all, what would you say of him? Might he be called perfectly virtuous?" The Master said, "He is more than a man of perfect virtue. He must be a sage! Even Yao and Shun[1] would find it hard to do. The man of perfect virtue is one who, desiring to sustain himself, sustains others, and desiring to develop himself, develops others. To be able to draw from one's self a parellel for the treatment of others, that may be called the way to practice virtue."

BOOK VII SHU ER

7.1 The Master said, "A transmitter and not an originator, believing in and loving the ancients, I venture to compare myself with Lao Peng."

7.2 The Master said, "To treasure up knowledge in silence, to learn without satiety and to instruct others without weariness---what one of these things have I done?"

---

① Two legendary emperors of the golden age.

7·3 子曰:“德之不修,學之不講,聞義不能徙,不善不能改,是吾憂也。”

【譯文】孔子說:“品德不培養,學問不講習,知道義的道理卻不能按義的要求去做,有缺點不能改正,這是我的憂慮。”

7·4 子之燕居,申申如也,夭夭如也。

【譯文】孔子在家閑居,穿戴整齊,和樂而舒展。

7·5 子曰:“甚矣吾衰也!久矣吾不復夢見周公!”

【譯文】孔子說:“我衰老得多麼厲害呀!我好長時間沒再夢見周公了!”

7·6 子曰:“志於道,據於德,依於仁,遊於藝。”

【譯文】孔子說:“目標在‘道’,根據在‘德’,依靠在‘仁’,遊習於禮、樂、射、御、書、數六藝之中。”

7·7 子曰:“自行束脩以上,吾未嘗無誨焉。”

【譯文】孔子說:“只要是主動地給我一點拜師薄禮,我從沒有不教誨的。”

7·8 子曰:“不憤不啓,不悱不發。舉一隅不以三隅反,則不復也。”

【譯文】孔子說:“不到他想求明白而感到困難的時候,不去開導他;不到他想說出來而說不明白的時候,不去啟發他。教給他東方,他卻不能由此推知另外三方,便不再教他了。”

7·9 子食於有喪者之側,未嘗飽也。

【譯文】孔子在死了親屬的人旁邊吃飯,從不曾吃飽過。

7. 3 The Master said, "Not to cultivate virtue, not to review what is learned, not to do the righteous though having heard of it, not to rectify what is not good---these things are what I worry about."

7. 4 When the Master was at home unoccupied, he was neatly dressed, and looked relaxed and cheerful.

7. 5 The Master said, "How deep is my decay! It is long since I saw the Duke of Zhou[①] in my dream."

7. 6 The Master said, "Set your heart on the Truth, hold to virtue, lean upon human-heartedness, and seek relaxation and enjoyment in the six arts.[②]"

7. 7 The Master said, "I have never refused instruction to any one, so long as he brought me no better present than a bundle of dried meat."

7. 8 The Master said, "Not until he is eager to know but feels difficulty do I instruct; not until he wants to speak out but fails to express himself do I enlighten. If I present him one corner and he cannot from it infer the other three, I do not continue the lesson."

7. 9 When the Master was eating by the side of a mourner, he never ate his fill.

---

① The younger brother of King Wu, the founder of the Zhou dynasty.

② Rites, music, archery, driving of chariot, learning and mathematics.

7·10　子於是日哭，則不歌。

【譯文】孔子在這一天哭泣過，就不再唱歌了。

7·11　子謂顏淵曰："用之則行，舍之則藏，惟我與爾有是夫！"

子路曰："子行三軍，則誰與？"

子曰："暴虎馮河，死而無悔者，吾不與也。必也臨事而懼，好謀而成者也。"

【譯文】孔子對顏淵說："用我，就幹起來；不用呢，就藏起來。只有我和你才能這樣吧！"

子路問："您若率領軍隊，找誰共事？"

孔子說："赤手空拳去和老虎搏斗，不用船隻去渡河，這樣死了都不後悔的人，我不和他共事。我要共事的一定是面對工作小心謹慎，講究謀略而能辦成事情的人。"

7·12　子曰："富而可求也，雖執鞭之士，吾亦爲之。如不可求，從吾所好。"

【譯文】孔子說："財富如果可以求得，雖然是拿着鞭子做市場的守門卒，我也去幹。如果不可以求得，還是幹我喜歡的事情。"

7·13　子之所慎：齋，戰，疾。

【譯文】孔子所小心謹慎的是：齋戒，戰爭，疾病。

7·14　子在齊聞《韶》，三月不知肉味，曰："不圖爲樂之至於斯也。"

【譯文】孔子在齊國聽到《韶》的樂章，很長時間嘗不出肉味。

7. 10 The Master did not sing on the same day in which he had been weeping.

7. 11 The Master said to Yan Yuan, "When wanted, then go; When set aside, then hide, —only you and I can attain to this."

Zilu asked, "If you had command of the army, whom would you like to take with you?"

The Master said, "I would not take such a man who will attack a tiger unarmed, or cross a river without a boat, not caring whether he lived or died. I should take the man who acts with caution and can succeed by strategy."

7. 12 The Master said, "If wealth can be obtained according to the Way, even though I should become a groom with a whip in hand to get it, I will do so. If it cannot be obtained according to the Way, then I will follow what I love."

7. 13 The things which the Master showed his greatest caution about were: fasting, war and sickness.

7. 14 When the Master was in Qi, he heard the Shao, and for three months did not know the taste of meat. He said, "I

他說："想不到音樂的美竟達到了這種境界。"

7·15 冉有曰："夫子爲衛君乎？"子貢曰："諾，吾將問之。"

入，曰："伯夷、叔齊何人也？"曰："古之賢人也。"曰："怨乎？"曰："求仁而得仁，又何怨？"

出，曰："夫子不爲也。"

【譯文】冉有說："老師幫助衛君嗎？"子貢說："好吧，我去問問他。"

子貢進到孔子屋裏，說："伯夷、叔齊是什麼樣的人？"孔子說："是古代的賢人。"子貢說："他們互相推讓，不肯做國君，都跑到國外，是不是後來又怨悔呢？"孔子說："他們求仁德而得到了仁德，又怨悔什麼呢？"

子貢走出來，答覆冉有說："老師不會幫助衛君。"

7·16 子曰："飯疏食飲水，曲肱而枕之，樂亦在其中矣。不義而富且貴，於我如浮雲。"

【譯文】孔子說："吃粗糧，喝冷水，彎着胳膊做枕頭，樂在其中。幹不正當的事而得來的富貴，對我來說好像浮雲。"

7·17 子曰："加我數年，五十以學《易》，可以無大過矣。"

【譯文】孔子說："讓我多活幾年，五十歲時去學習《易》，便可以沒有大過錯了。"

7·18 子所雅言，《詩》、《書》、執禮，皆雅言也。

【譯文】孔子有用普通話的時候，讀《詩》，讀《書》，行禮，都用普通話。

7·19 葉公問孔子於子路，子路不對。子曰："女奚不曰，其

have not expected that music could reach such perfection as this."

7.15 Ran You said, "Is our Master will help the prince of Wei?" Zigong said, "I'll ask him."

He went in and said, "What sort of people were Boyi and Shuqi?" The Master said, "They were ancient worthies." Zigong said, "Did they have any repentance?" The Master replied, "They sought perfect virtue and they got it. What did they repent of?"

Zigong came out and said, "Our Master will not help him."

7.16 The Master said, "With coarse food to eat, with water to drink, and my bent arm for a pillow, I still have joy in these things. Wealth and honours obtained by unrighteousness are to me as floating clouds."

7.17 The Master said, "Add a few more years to my life, I will study the Book of Changes when I reach age fifty. Then I may fairly free from errors."

7.18 The Master used the standard language when reading the Book of Poetry or the Book of History and when practising the ritual acts.

7.19 The Duke of She asked Zilu about Confucius, Zilu

爲人也，發憤忘食，樂以忘憂，不知老之將至云爾。”

【譯文】葉公向子路問孔子為人怎么樣，子路不回答。孔子對子路說：“你為什么不這樣說：他的為人，發憤用功，連吃飯也忘了，快樂得忘記了憂愁，不曉得衰老即將到來，如此罷了。”

7·20 子曰：“我非生而知之者，好古，敏以求之者也。”

【譯文】孔子說：“我不是生下來就有知識的人，而是喜歡古代文化，勤快地去追求的人。”

7·21 子不語怪、力、亂、神。

【譯文】孔子不談論怪異、勇力、叛亂和鬼神。

7·22 子曰：“三人行，必有我師焉。擇其善者而從之，其不善者而改之。”

【譯文】孔子說：“三個人同行，其中就一定有我的老師。我選擇他善的品德向他學習，并把他的缺點作為借鑒改掉自己的不足。”

7·23 子曰：“天生德於予，桓魋其如予何？”

【譯文】孔子說：“上天賦予我這樣的品德，桓魋將把我怎麼樣？”

7·24 子曰：“二三子以我爲隱乎？吾無隱乎爾。吾無行而不與二三子者，是丘也。”

【譯文】孔子說：“你們這些學生以為我對你們有所隱瞞嗎？我没有隱瞞。我没有什么不告訴你們的，這是我孔丘的為人。”

7·25 子以四教：文，行，忠，信。

did not answer him. The Master said, "Why did you not say: he is simply a man who in his eager pursuit of knowledge forgets to eat, who is so happy that he forgets his sorrow, and does not realize that old age is coming on?"

7.20 The Master said, "I am not one who was born with innate knowledge. I am simply one who loves ancient culture and who is diligent in seeking it."

7.21 The Master never talked of extraordinary things, feats of strength, disorder or spiritual beings.

7.22 The Master said, "When three are walking together, I am sure to find teachers among them. I will select their good qualities and follow them, their bad qualities and avoid them."

7.23 The Master said, "Heaven bestowed the virtue on me, What can Huan Tui① do to me?"

7.24 The Master said, "My disciples, do you think I conceal things from you? I conceal nothing. I have nothing that I would not show to you, my disciples, ---this is my way."

7.25 The four things the Master taught were historical

---

① An officer of Song. He once tried to kill Confucius.

【譯文】孔子以文、行、忠、信四項内容教育學生。

7·26 子曰:“聖人,吾不得而見之矣;得見君子者,斯可矣。”

子曰:“善人,吾不得而見之矣;得見有恒者,斯可矣。亡而爲有,虚而爲盈,約而爲泰,難乎有恒矣。”

【譯文】孔子説:“聖人,我不能看到他了,能看到君子,就可以了。”

孔子説:“善人,我不能看見了,能看見有一定操守的人,就可以了。没有卻裝做有,空虛卻裝做充足,窮困卻裝做富有,這樣的人便難於保持一定操守了。”

7·27 子釣而不綱,弋不射宿。

【譯文】孔子釣魚,但不用大魚網捕魚;射鳥不射歸巢歇宿的鳥。

7·28 子曰:“蓋有不知而作之者,我無是也。多聞,擇其善者而從之;多見而識之;知之次也。”

【譯文】孔子説:“大概有一種自己不懂卻憑空造作的人,我没有這種毛病。多多地聽,選擇其中的合理部分加以接受;多多地看,全記在心裏。這種求知的方法僅次於生而知之。”

7·29 互鄉難與言,童子見,門人惑。子曰:“與其進也,不與其退也,唯何甚?人潔己以進,與其潔也,不保其往也。”

【譯文】互鄉這地方的人難於和他們交談,一個童子得到孔子的接見,弟子們疑惑不解。孔子説:“我贊成他的進步,不贊成他的退步,何必做得太過分。别人把自己弄得乾乾淨淨而來,應該贊成他乾淨的一面,不要死記住他的過去。”

records, conduct, faithfulness and honesty.

7.26 The Master said, "A sage I will not live to see; enough could I find a man of virtue!"

The Master said, "A good man I will not live to see; enough could I find a man of consistency! Nothing and yet pretending to be something, empty and yet pretending to be full, poor and yet pretending to be rich:---men with such characteristics are difficult to have consistency."

7.27 The Master fished with a hook but not with a net. He shot, but not at roosting birds.

7.28 The Master said, "There may be those who can do without knowledge. I am not one of them. To hear much, pick out the good and follow it; to see much, and keep it in memory: this comes next to innate knowledge."

7.29 It is hard to talk with the people of Huxiang. When a lad of that place had an interview with the Master, the disciples wondered. The Master said, "I approve of his progress, and I disapprove of his regression. Why be so severe? If a man purifies himself to come to us, I approve of his purification and will not always keep his past in mind."

7·30 子曰："仁遠乎哉？我欲仁，斯仁至矣。"

【譯文】孔子說："仁德距離我們遠嗎？我想要做到仁德，仁德就來到了。"

7·31 陳司敗問："昭公知禮乎？"孔子曰："知禮。"

孔子退，揖巫馬期而進之，曰："吾聞君子不黨，君子亦黨乎？君取於吳，爲同姓，謂之吳孟子。君而知禮，孰不知禮？"

巫馬期以告。子曰："丘也幸，苟有過，人必知之。"

【譯文】陳司敗問孔子："魯昭公懂不懂禮法？"孔子說："懂禮法。"

孔子走了出來，陳司敗便向巫馬期作了個揖，請他走近自己，說："我聽說君子無所偏袒，難道孔子竟偏袒嗎？魯君從吳國娶了位夫人，吳和魯是同姓國家，不便叫她吳姬，於是叫她吳孟子。魯君若是懂得禮法，誰不懂得禮法呢？"

巫馬期把這話告訴了孔子。孔子說："我真幸運，假若有錯誤，別人一定知道。"

7·32 子與人歌而善，必使反之，而後和之。

【譯文】孔子同別人一道唱歌，別人唱得好，一定請他再唱一遍，然後跟着他唱。

7·33 子曰："文，莫吾猶人也。躬行君子，則吾未之有得。"

【譯文】孔子說："文獻知識，大概我同別人差不多。親身實踐，做一個君子，那我還沒有做到。"

7·34 子曰："若聖與仁，則吾豈敢？抑爲之不厭，誨人不倦，則可謂云爾已矣。"公西華曰："正唯弟子不能學也。"

7. 30 The Master said, "Is virtue indeed far off? I crave for virtue, and Lo! Virtue is at hand!"

7. 31 Chen Sibai asked whether the duke Zhao ① knew propriety. Confucius said, "He knew propriety."

Wen Confucius had left, Chen bowed to Wuma Qi② to come forward and said, "I have heard that the superior man is never partial. May the superior man be partial also? The prince married a Wu, of the same surname as himself③, and called her Wu Meng Zi. If the prince knew propriety, who does not know it?"

When Wuma Qi told this to the Master, he said, "I am so lucky! If I have any errors, people are sure to know it!"

7. 32 When anyone sang to the Master, and sang well, he would make him repeat it and join in.

7. 33 The Master said, "As for cultural knowledge, perhaps I am equal to other men, but as to carrying out the duties of a superior man in actual life, I have not yet attained."

7. 34 The Master said, "As to being a sage or a man of perfect virtue, how dare I lay any such claim? It may simply be

---

① A duke of Lu.

② A disciple of Confucius.

③ According to the rules of propriety, a man should not marry a girl of the same surname as himself.

【譯文】孔子說:"講到聖和仁,我怎麼敢當?不過是工作不厭倦,教導別人不疲勞,就是如此罷了。"公西華說:"這正是學生們學不到的。"

7·35 子疾病,子路請禱。子曰:"有諸?"子路對曰:"有之。《誄》曰:'禱爾于上下神祇。'"子曰:"丘之禱久矣。"

【譯文】孔子病重,子路請求祈禱。孔子說:"有這回事嗎?"子路回答說:"有的。《誄》文說過:'為你在天神地祇前祈禱。'"孔子說:"我早就祈禱過了。"

7·36 子曰:"奢則不孫,儉則固。與其不孫也,寧固。"

【譯文】孔子說:"奢侈就顯得驕傲,儉省就顯得寒傖。與其驕傲,寧可寒傖。"

7·37 子曰:"君子坦蕩蕩,小人長戚戚。"

【譯文】孔子說:"君子心地平坦寬廣,小人經常局促憂愁。"

7·38 子溫而厲,威而不猛,恭而安。

【譯文】孔子溫和而嚴厲,有威儀而不兇猛,莊嚴而安詳。

泰伯篇第八

8·1 子曰:"泰伯,其可謂至德也已矣。三以天下讓,民無得而稱焉。"

【譯文】孔子說:"泰伯,那可以說是品德極高尚了。屢次把天下讓給弟弟,老百姓找不出恰當的詞語來稱贊他。"

said of me that I learn without unflagging efforts and teach others without weariness." Gongxi Hua said, "This is just what we disciples cannot learn."

7.35 When the Master was very ill, Zilu asked leave to pray for him. The Master said, "Is there such a thing?" Zilu answered, "There is. In the Prayers it is said, 'Pray to the spirits in Heaven above and on earth below!'" The Master said, "My praying began long ago!"

7.36 The Master said, "Extravagance leads to arrogance; frugality leads to meanness: but it is better to be mean than to be arrogant."

7.37 The superior man is always calm and at ease, the small man is always fretting.

7.38 The Master was mild, yet dignified; awe-inspiring but kind at heart; respectful but easy.

BOOK VIII TAI BO

8.1 The Master said, "Taibo[1] may indeed be called a man of highest virtue. Thrice he abdicated the throne to his younger brother. The people could not find proper words to praise him for it."

---

① Taibo was the eldest son of Gugong Danfu, legendary ancestor of the Zhou sovereigns. The father wished his third son to succeed him, in order that the throne might pass through him to his famous son, afterwards known as king Wen. To facilitate this plan Taibo and his second brother went into voluntary exile.

8·2　子曰:“恭而無禮則勞,慎而無禮則葸,勇而無禮則亂,直而無禮則絞。君子篤於親,則民興於仁;故舊不遺,則民不偷。”

【譯文】孔子說:“恭敬而不知禮法就會辛勞,謹慎而不知禮法就會膽小怕事,勇敢而不知禮法就會作亂,心直口快而不知禮法就會尖刻刺人。統治者能用深厚感情對待親族,老百姓就會走向仁德;統治者不遺棄他的老同事和老朋友,百姓就不致對人冷淡無情。”

8·3　曾子有疾,召門弟子曰:“啓予足,啓予手,《詩》云:‘戰戰兢兢,如臨深淵,如履薄冰。’而今而後,吾知免夫! 小子!”

【譯文】曾參病了,把他的學生召集來說:“看看我的腳,看看我的手,《詩經》上說:‘謹慎得戰戰兢兢,好像面臨深淵,好像行走在薄冰上。’從今以后,我知道自己可以免於禍患刑戮了!學生們!”

8·4　曾子有疾,孟敬子問之。曾子言曰:“鳥之將死,其鳴也哀;人之將死,其言也善。君子所貴乎道者三:動容貌,斯遠暴慢矣;正顏色,斯近信矣;出辭氣,斯遠鄙倍矣。籩豆之事,則有司存。”

【譯文】曾參病了,孟敬子探問他。曾子說:“鳥要死了,鳴聲是悲哀的;人要死了,說出的話是善意的。在上位的人應重視的儀容態度有三方面:容貌莊嚴,就可以避免招來粗暴和怠慢;臉色端正,就接近於誠信;言辭得體,就可以避免鄙陋和錯誤。至於禮儀的細節,自有主管人員去安排。”

8·5　曾子曰:“以能問於不能,以多問於寡,有若無,實若虛,犯而不校,昔者吾友嘗從事於斯矣。”

8. 2 The Master said, "Respectfulness, without the rules of propriety, becomes fussiness; caution, without the rules of propriety, becomes timidity; daring, without the rules of propriety, becomes turbulance; straightforwardness, without the rules of propriety, becomes harshness. When the ruler deals generously with his own kinsmen, the people will be incited to human-heartedness. If he does not discard his old friends, the people will not be fickle."

8. 3 When Zeng Zi was sick, he summoned his disciples and said, "Look at my feet, look at my hands. The Book of Poetry says, 'Be apprehensive and cautious, as if on the brink of a deep gulf, as if treading on thin ice.' From now on I know I will escape from all injury, my disciples."

8. 4 Zeng Zi being sick, Meng Jing Zi ① came to ask after him. Zeng Zi said, "When a bird is about to die, its notes are mourn ful; when a man is about to die, his words are true. There are three principles of conduct which the man of high rank should consider specially important: adopt a solemn attitude and manner to keep from violence and levity; regulate his countenance to keep near to sincerity; utter proper words to avoid coarseness and impropriety. As for temple matters, there are officers in charge mind them."

8. 5 Zeng Zi said, "Gifted with ability, and yet consulting those who were not so; possessing much, and yet consulting

---

① Head of the Meng clan, high official of Lu.

【譯文】曾子說："自己有能力卻向沒有能力的人請教，自己知識豐富卻向知識缺少的人請教，有學問卻像沒有學問的人一樣，滿腹知識卻像空無所有的人一樣，受到觸犯而不計較。從前我的一位朋友便曾這樣做了。"

8·6 曾子曰："可以託六尺之孤，可以寄百里之命，臨大節而不可奪也，君子人與？君子人也。"

【譯文】曾子說："可以把幼小的孤兒托付給他，可以把方圓百里的國家委托給他，遇到緊要關頭能保持着自己的節操，這種人是君子人嗎？是君子啊。"

8·7 曾子曰："士不可以不弘毅，任重而道遠。仁以爲己任，不亦重乎？死而後已，不亦遠乎？"

【譯文】曾子說："讀書人不可以不剛強而有毅力，他責任重大，路程遙遠。以實現仁德為自己的任務，責任不是很重大嗎？到死才停下來，路程不也遙遠嗎？"

8·8 子曰："興於《詩》，立於禮，成於樂。"

【譯文】孔子說："（人的修養）開始於學《詩》，自立于學禮，完成於學樂。"

8·9 子曰："民可使由之，不可使知之。"

【譯文】孔子說："百姓可以使他們照着指點的道路走去，不可以使他們知道那是為什麼。"

8·10 子曰："好勇疾貧，亂也。人而不仁，疾之已甚，亂也。"

【譯文】孔子說："喜好勇力而又厭惡貧窮，就會作亂。對於不

those who possessed little; having, yet seeming as not to have; full, yet seeming empty; offended against, and yet never contesting: I had once a friend who pursued such conduct."

8. 6 Zeng Zi said, "A man who may be entrusted to a young orphan prince or the fate of the one-hundred-Li state; who is in the moment of crisis still holds to his principles---is such a man not a superior man? A superior man indeed!"

8. 7 Zeng Zi said, "The scholar may not have no broad-mind or vigorous endurance. His burden is heavy and his road is long. To practise virtue is the burden he takes upon him, is it not heavy? Only with death does his road stop, is it not long?"

8. 8 The Master said, "By the Book of Poetry a man is first incited; in the rules of propriety he takes his stand; and finally by music he is perfected."

8. 9 The Master said, "The people may be made to follow our will, but they may not be made to understand it."

8. 10 The Master said, "The man who is fond of daring and is inflamed with poverty, may proceed to insubordination. The man who is not virtuous and is deeply ill-treated, will turn

仁的人痛恨太過分,也會出亂子。”

8·11 子曰:“如有周公之才之美,使驕且吝,其餘不足觀也已。”

【譯文】孔子說:“假如有周公那樣美好的才能,如果他驕傲而吝嗇,別的方面也就不值一顧了。”

8·12 子曰:“三年學,不至於穀,不易得也。”

【譯文】孔子說:“讀書三年,無意於作官得俸祿,這種人是難得的。”

8·13 子曰:“篤信好學,守死善道。危邦不入,亂邦不居。天下有道則見,無道則隱。邦有道,貧且賤焉,恥也;邦無道,富且貴焉,恥也。”

【譯文】孔子說:“堅定地相信道,努力學習它,誓死保衛,使它完善。不進入危險的國家,不居住混亂的國家。天下清平就出來作官,腐敗黑暗就隱居。政治清明,自己貧賤,是恥辱;政治黑暗,自己富貴,也是恥辱。”

8·14 子曰:“不在其位,不謀其政。”

【譯文】孔子說:“不在那個職位,就不考慮那方面的工作。”

8·15 子曰:“師摯之始,《關雎》之亂,洋洋乎盈耳哉!”

【譯文】孔子說:“當太師摯開始演奏的時候,當演奏完《關雎》的時候,悠揚的樂聲充耳呀!”

8·16 子曰:“狂而不直,侗而不願,悾悾而不信,吾不知之矣。”

to insubordination too."

8.11 The Master said, "Though a man has gifts as glorious as those of the Duke of Zhou, if he is arrogant and mean, all the rest is worthless of even one glance."

8.12 The Master said, "It is hard to find a man who has studied for three years without thought of emolument."

8.13 The Master said, "Show unwaving faith in the Way, study it hard and be ready to die in defending and perfecting it. Do not enter a tottering state, nor stay in a disorganized one. When the Way prevails in the world, come out and take office; when it does not prevail, keep concealed. When the Way prevails in the state, count it a disgrace to be needy and lowly; When the Way does not prevail in the state, then count it a disgrace to be rich and honoured."

8.14 The Master said, "He who holds no rank in a state discusses no policies."

8.15 The Master said, "From the music master Zhi began to play till the final strains of Guan Ju, what melodious music filled my ears!"

8.16 The Master said, "Ardent, but not upright; shallow, but not simple; dull, but not truthful---such persons I re-

【譯文】孔子說："狂妄而不直率，幼稚而不樸實，無知而不講信用，我無法理解這種人。"

8・17 子曰："學如不及，猶恐失之。"

【譯文】孔子說："做學問好像追逐什麽，生怕追不上；追上了，又生怕丢掉了。"

8・18 子曰："巍巍乎，舜、禹之有天下也而不與焉！"

【譯文】孔子說："舜和禹真是崇高啊！擁有天下而不為自己。"

8・19 子曰："大哉堯之爲君也！巍巍乎！唯天爲大，唯堯則之。蕩蕩乎，民無能名焉。巍巍乎其有成功也，焕乎其有文章！"

【譯文】孔子說："堯作為國君真偉大啊！崇高啊！只有天最高大，唯獨堯能夠效法天。他的恩惠廣博無邊，老百姓不知道怎樣去稱贊他。他的功業真是崇高啊！他的禮儀制度也太美好了！"

8・20 舜有臣五人而天下治。武王曰："予有亂臣十人。"孔子曰："才難，不其然乎？唐虞之際，於斯爲盛。有婦人焉，九人而已。三分天下有其二，以服事殷。周之德，其可謂至德也已矣。"

【譯文】舜有五位賢臣，便天下太平。武王說："我有十位能治理天下的臣子。"孔子說："人才不易得。不是這樣嗎？唐堯虞舜之際，周武王說那話的時候，人才最興盛。那十人中還有一位婦女，實際上只是九人。周文王得了天下的三分之二，仍然向商紂稱臣，周朝的道德，可以說是至高無上了。"

8・21 子曰："禹，吾無間然矣。菲飲食而致孝乎鬼神，惡衣服而致美乎黻冕，卑宫室而盡力乎溝洫。禹，吾無間然矣。"

ally do not understand."

8.17 The Master said, "Learn as if you were following something to which you can never catch up, as if you were in fear of losing what you have got."

8.18 The Master said, "Sublime indeed were Shun and Yu! They held possession of the whole world, but did nothing for themselves."

8.19 The Master said, "How great was Yao as a sovereign! How sublime! Heaven alone is great; Yao alone corresponded to it. Boundless! The people could find no proper words to praise him. Sublime were his achievements! Glorious the regulations he instituted!"

8.20 Shun had five ministers, and the empire was well governed. King Wu said, "I have ten able ministers." Confucius said, "It is difficult to find the talents. Is that not true? Only the times of Tang Yao and Yu Shun and the time of King Wu were rich in talents. There was a woman among King Wu's ten talents. So there were but nine talents in all. King Wu possessed two of the three parts of the world, and with these he served the dynasty of Yin. The utmost virtue was the virtue of Zhou!"

8.21 The Master said, "I find no flaw in Yu. He used himself coarse food and drink, but he displayed the utmost de-

【譯文】孔子說："禹，我對他沒有意見了。他吃得很差，卻對鬼神祭祀很豐盛；穿得很壞，卻把祭祀的衣冠做得極華美；住得很簡陋，卻把力量完全用於溝渠水利。禹，我對他沒有意見了。"

子罕篇第九

9·1 子罕言利與命與仁。

【譯文】孔子很少談到功利、命運和仁德。

9·2 達巷黨人曰："大哉孔子！博學而無所成名。"子聞之，謂門弟子曰："吾何執？執御乎？執射乎？吾執御矣。"

【譯文】達街的一個人說："孔子真偉大！學問廣博，可惜沒有足以樹立名聲的專長。"孔子聽了這話，就對學生們說："我幹什麼呢？趕馬車嗎？做射箭手嗎？我趕馬車好了。"

9·3 子曰："麻冕，禮也；今也純，儉，吾從衆。拜下，禮也；今拜乎上，泰也。雖違衆，吾從下。"

【譯文】孔子說："用麻織禮帽，合乎傳統的禮儀；今天大家都用黑絲，儉省，我贊成大家的做法。臣子朝見君主，先在堂下磕頭，合乎傳統的禮儀。現在升堂後磕頭，是倨傲的表現。雖然與衆不同，我仍然要先在堂下磕頭。"

9·4 子絶四：毋意，毋必，毋固，毋我。

【譯文】孔子沒有四種毛病：不憑空揣測，不絕對肯定，不拘泥固執，不唯我獨是。

9·5 子畏於匡，曰："文王既沒，文不在兹乎？天之將喪斯

votion in his offerings to the spirits and divinities. His common wear was poor, but he displayed the utmost elegance in his sacrificial cap and apron. He lived in a humble house, but expended all his strength on draining and ditching. In him I can find no flaw."

BOOK IX ZI HAN

9. 1 The Master seldom spoke of profit or fate or human-heartedness.

9. 2 A man of Daxiang said, "Great indeed is the Master Kong! His learning is extensive, and yet he has no speciality to render his name famous." When the Master heard this he said to his disciples, "What shall I take up? Shall I take up chariot-driving? Or shall I take up archery? I think I will take up chariot-driving!"

9. 3 The Master said, "A linen cap is prescribed by the rules of ceremony, but now a silk one is worn. It is economical, and I follow the general practice. To bow below the hall is prescribed by the rules of ceremony, but now it is done after ascending the hall. This is presumptuous. I still bow below the hall, though to do so is contrary to the general practice."

9. 4 From four things the Master was entirely free. He made no arbitrary conjectures. He was never over-positive, never obstinate, never egotistic.

9. 5 When the Master was trapped in Kuang, he said,

文也，后死者不得與於斯文也；天之未喪斯文也，匡人其如予何？”

【譯文】孔子被匡地的群衆所拘禁，便說：“周文王死了以後，一切文化遺產不都在我這裏嗎？天若是要消滅這些文化，那我也不會掌握這些文化了；天若是不想消滅這些文化，那匡人將把我怎麼樣呢？”

9·6 太宰問於子貢曰：“夫子聖者與？何其多能也？”子貢曰：“固天縱之將聖，又多能也。”

子聞之，曰：“太宰知我乎？吾少也賤，故多能鄙事。君子多乎哉？不多也。”

【譯文】太宰問子貢說：“孔老夫子是聖人嗎？為什麼這樣多才多藝呢？”子貢說：“這本是上天讓他成為聖人，又使他多才多藝。”

孔子聽到了，便說：“太宰瞭解我嗎？我小時候窮苦，所以學會了不少鄙賤的技藝。君子會有這樣多的技巧嗎？是不會有很多的。”

9·7 牢曰：“子云：‘吾不試，故藝。’”

【譯文】琴牢說：“孔子說過：‘我不曾被國家所用，所以學得一些技藝。’”

9·8 子曰：“吾有知乎哉？無知也。有鄙夫問於我，空空如也。我叩其兩端而竭焉。”

【譯文】孔子說：“我有知識嗎？沒有啊。有一個莊稼漢問我，我一點也不知道。我從他那個問題的始末去盤問，得到啟發，然後儘量地回答他。”

"Since the death of King Wen, was not all ancient culture (Wen) lodged here in me? If Heaven had wished to let such culture perish, later generations (like myself) would not possess it. But since Heaven has not wished to let such culture perish, what can the people of Kuang do to me?"

9.6 A high minister asked Zigong, "Is your Master a sage? Why does he has various ability?" Zigong said, "Certainly Heaven intended him to become a sage and have various ability."

When the Master heard it, he said, "Does the minister know me? When I was young I was in humble circumstances. That is why I learned many an humble trade. But does a superior man have such variety of ability? No, he has few."

9.7 Lao said, "The Master said, 'Having no official employment, I acquired many arts.'"

9.8 The Master said, "Am I indeed possessed of knowledge? No! But if a simple peasant asked me a question, I am ready to thrash the matter out from one end to the other and exhaust it and then tell him as much as possible."

9·9 子曰:“鳳鳥不至,河不出圖,吾已矣夫!”

【譯文】孔子說:“鳳凰不飛來了,黄河也没有圖畫出來了,我這一生完了!”

9·10 子見齊衰者、冕衣裳者與瞽者,見之,雖少,必作;過之,必趨。

【譯文】孔子看見穿喪服的人、戴禮帽穿禮服的人和瞎了眼睛的人,相見的時候,他們雖然年輕,孔子一定站起來;走過的時候,一定快走幾步。

9·11 顏淵喟然歎曰:“仰之彌高,鑽之彌堅。瞻之在前,忽焉在後。夫子循循然善誘人,博我以文,約我以禮,欲罷不能。既竭吾才,如有所立卓爾。雖欲從之,末由也已。”

【譯文】顏淵長長地感歎說:“老師之道,抬頭仰望,越望越覺得高;鑽研着,越鑽研越覺得深。看它在前面,忽然又到後面去了。老師善於有步驟地誘導我們,用各種文獻豐富我們的知識,用禮法約束我們的行為,使我們想停止學習都不可能。我已經用盡我的才能,像是見到了它高高地矗立在面前,我雖然想要追隨上去,卻没有前進的路徑了。”

9·12 子疾病,子路使門人爲臣。病間,曰:“久矣哉,由之行詐也!無臣而爲有臣。吾誰欺?欺天乎!且予與其死於臣之手也,無寧死於二三子之手乎!且予縱不得大葬,予死於道路乎!”

【譯文】孔子病得厲害,子路便讓孔子的學生做家臣為孔子準備後事。過了一段時間,孔子的病漸漸好了,便說:“仲由幹這種欺假勾當太長久了!没有家臣而裝做有家臣。我欺騙誰呢?欺騙上天嗎?我與其死在家臣的手裏,寧肯死在你們學生的手裏。

9. 9 The Master said, "The phoenix does not come, the Yellow River gives forth no chart①. It is all over with me."

9. 10 When the Master saw a person in a mourning dress, or in robes of state, or a blind person, he would always rise up, though they were younger than himself; and if he was passing by them, he would always quicken his steps. ②

9. 11 Yan Yuan said with a deep sigh, "The more I look up to the Master's doctrine, the higher it soars. The deeper I bore down into it, the harder it becomes. I see it before me, and suddenly it seemed to be behind. The Master skillfully leads me on step by step. He has broadened me with culture and restrained me with the rules of propriety. When I want to stop learning, I cannot do so. Having exerted all my ability, there seems something to stand right up before me; but though I long to follow and reach it, I can find no way to do so."

9. 12 When the Master was very ill, Zilu had some disciples to act as retainers to prepare for funeral affairs. During a better spell the Master said, "Long has the conduct of Zhong You been deceitful! By pretending to have retainers when I have none, whom do I deceive? Do I deceive Heaven? Moreover, is it not better to die in the hands of you disciples than to die in the hands of retainers? And if I may not have a grand burial,

---

① The arrival of this magical bird and the sudden revelation of a magical chart were porents that heralded the rise of a Saviour Sage.

② A sign of respect.

我縱不能熱熱鬧鬧地辦理喪葬，難道會死在路上嗎？”

9·13 子貢曰：“有美玉於斯，韞匵而藏諸？求善賈而沽諸？”子曰：“沽之哉！沽之哉！我待賈者也。”

【譯文】子貢說：“這裏有一塊美玉，把它放在櫃子裏藏起來呢？還是找一個識貨的人賣掉呢？”孔子說：“賣掉，賣掉！我在等待識貨的人。”

9·14 子欲居九夷。或曰：“陋，如之何？”子曰：“君子居之，何陋之有？”

【譯文】孔子想搬到九夷去住。有人說：“那地方非常簡陋，怎麼行？”孔子說：“有君子去住，有什么簡陋呢？”

9·15 子曰：“吾自衛反魯，然後樂正，《雅》《頌》各得其所。”

【譯文】孔子說：“我從衛國回到魯國，然後《詩》的樂章得到訂正，《雅》歸《雅》，《頌》歸《頌》，各有適當的地方。”

9·16 子曰：“出則事公卿，入則事父兄，喪事不敢不勉，不爲酒困，何有於我哉？”

【譯文】孔子說：“出外便服事公卿，入門便服事父兄，有喪事不敢不竭盡其力，不被酒所困擾，我做到了哪些呢？”

9·17 子在川上，曰：“逝者如斯夫！不舍晝夜。”

【譯文】孔子在河邊，說：“一去不返的光陰如同這河水啊，日日夜夜不停地流去。”

9·18 子曰：“吾未見好德如好色者也。”

shall I die by the roadside?"

9.13 Zigong said, "Suppose there was a beautiful jade here, should I hide it away in a case, or seek a good price and sell it?" The Master said, "Sell it! Sell it! I am waiting for a man who really appreciates it."

9.14 The Master wanted to go and live among the nine wild tribes of the east. Someone said, "That place is very poor. How can you do such a thing?" The Master said, "If a superior man lived there, what poverty would there be?"

9.15 The Master said, "Only after I came back from Wei to Lu, was the music reformed and were the pieces in the Imperial Songs (Ya) and Praise Songs (Song) properly sorted and given their proper places."

9.16 The Master said, "Abroad, to serve the high officers; at home, to serve one's father and brothers; to do the utmost in the funeral and not to be overcome with wine---what one of these things do I attain to?"

9.17 Standing by a stream, the Master said, "Time passes on just like the flowing water in the river, not ceasing day or night!"

9.18 The Master said, "I have not seen one who loves

【譯文】孔子說："我沒有看見過喜愛道德好像喜愛美色一樣的人。"

9·19 子曰："譬如爲山，未成一簣，止，吾止也。譬如平地，雖覆一簣，進，吾往也。"

【譯文】孔子說："好比堆土成山，只差一筐土沒有成山，便停止了，這是我自己停止的。又好比在平地上堆土成山，即使剛剛倒下一筐土，仍要努力前進，那也是我自己前進。"

9·20 子曰："語之而不惰者，其回也與！"

【譯文】孔子說："聽我說話始終不懈怠的，大概只顏回一個人吧！"

9·21 子謂顏淵，曰："惜乎！吾見其進也，未見其止也。"

【譯文】孔子談到顏淵，說道："他死了可惜呀！我只看見他進步，從沒看見他停滯不前。"

9·22 子曰："苗而不秀者有矣夫！秀而不實者有矣夫！"

【譯文】孔子說："莊稼不吐穗開花的有過的吧！吐穗開花卻不結實的有過的吧！"

9·23 子曰："後生可畏，焉知來者之不如今也？四十、五十而無聞焉，斯亦不足畏也已。"

【譯文】孔子說："年輕人是可敬畏的，怎能斷定他們將來趕不上現在的人呢？四、五十歲還沒有什麼名望，也就值不得敬畏了。"

9·24 子曰："法語之言，能無從乎？改之爲貴。巽與之言，

virtue as he loves women."

9. 19 The Master said, "As in making a mound, if I stop when one more basket of earth would end it, it is I that stop. As in levelling ground, if I go on after throwing down only one basket of earth, it is I that proceed."

9. 20 The Master said, "It is only Hui who could never be flagging when I spoke anything to him."

9. 21 The Master said of Yan Yuan, "What a pity that he has died! I have seen him go on, but never have I seen him stop."

9. 22 The Master said, "There are sprouts which can spring up but never flower; there are others which can flower but never bear fruit."

9. 23 The Master said, "Awe is due to the youth. How do we know that their future will not be equal to our present? To men of forty or fifty, who have not made themselves heard of yet, no awe is due."

9. 24 The Master said, "Who would not give ear to the

能無說乎？繹之爲貴。說而不繹，從而不改，吾末如之何也已矣。”

【譯文】孔子說：“合於禮法的正言規勸，能夠不接受嗎？改正錯誤才可貴。順從自己的話，能夠不高興嗎？分析研究一下才可貴。只高興，不加分析研究，表面接受，實際不改，這種人我是沒有辦法對付他的了。”

9·25 子曰：“主忠信，毋友不如己者，過則勿憚改。”

【譯文】孔子說：“應以忠心和信實兩種品德為主，不要跟不如自己的人交朋友，有了過錯就不要怕改正。”

9·26 子曰：“三軍可奪帥也，匹夫不可奪志也。”

【譯文】孔子說：“一個國家的軍隊，可以奪去它的主帥，一個普通人卻不可能強迫他改變志向。”

9·27 子曰：“衣敝緼袍，與衣狐貉者立，而不恥者，其由也與？‘不忮不求，何用不臧？’”子路終身誦之。子曰：“是道也，何足以臧？”

【譯文】孔子說：“穿着破爛的絲綿袍和穿着狐貉裘的人一道站着，不覺得慚愧的，恐怕只有仲由吧？《詩經》說‘不嫉妒，不貪求，為什么不會好？’”子路聽了，終生唸着這兩句詩。孔子說：“僅僅這個樣子，怎樣能夠好得起來？”

9·28 子曰：“歲寒，然後知松柏之後彫也。”

【譯文】孔子說：“季節寒冷了，才知道松柏樹是最後凋謝的。”

9·29 子曰：“知者不惑，仁者不憂，勇者不懼。”

【譯文】孔子說：“聰明人不致疑惑，仁德的人沒有憂愁，勇敢

strict words conforming to the rules of propriety? But to reform his conduct is praisable. Who would not be pleased by flattering words? But to ponder these words is praisable. With those who give ear but will not reform his conduct, who are pleased but will not ponder, I can really do nothing."

9.25 The Master said, "Hold faithfulness and sincerity as first principles. Do not make friends with those who are not as good as you. When you have faults, you must not fear to correct them."

9.26 The Master said, "The commander of the army may be carried off, but the will of even a common man cannot be taken from him."

9.27 The Master said, "Dressed in a tattered, quilted robe, standing by the side of men in furs, and yet not ashamed, it is only Zhong You who can do so. As it says in the Book of Poctry, 'Void of hatrcd and grccd, what clsc but good docs hc do?'" Afterwards Zilu kept on repeating these lines, the Master said, "Those things are by no means sufficient to constitute perfect excellence."

9.28 The Master said, "Only when the year becomes cold, do we know that the pine and cypress are the last to fade."

9.29 The Master said, "The wise are free from doubts; the virtuous from anxiety; and the brave from fear."

的人無所畏懼。”

9·30 子曰:“可與共學,未可與適道;可與適道,未可與立;可與立,未可與權。”

【譯文】孔子說:“可以在一起學習,但未必能一起走向道;可以一起走向道的,未必能一起堅持道而不變;可以一起堅持不變的,未必能一起權衡輕重、靈活處事。”

9·31 “唐棣之華,偏其反而。豈不爾思?室是遠而。”子曰:“未之思也,夫何遠之有?”

【譯文】“唐棣的花朵,翩翩搖擺。難道我不想念你?只因為家住得太遙遠。”孔子道:“你是不去想念,有什麽遥遠呢?”

鄉黨篇第十

10·1 孔子於鄉黨,恂恂如也,似不能言者。其在宗廟朝廷,便便言,唯謹爾。

【譯文】孔子在家鄉,非常恭順,好像不能說話的人。他在宗廟裏或朝廷上,便明白而流暢地說話,只是很謹慎罷了。

10·2 朝,與下大夫言,侃侃如也;與上大夫言,誾誾如也。君在,踧踖如也,與與如也。

【譯文】上朝廷,同下大夫說話,溫和而快樂的樣子;同上大夫說話,正直而恭敬的樣子。君主臨朝,恭敬而心中不安的樣子,行步安祥的樣子。

10·3 君召使擯,色勃如也,足躩如也。揖所與立,左右手,衣前後,襜如也。趨進,翼如也。賓退,必復命曰:“賓不顧矣。”

9. 30 The Master said, "With some we can join in learning, but not in the Way; with others we can join in the Way, but not in adhering to the Way; and with others again we can join in adhering to the Way, but not in weighing occurring events along with us."

9. 31 As a poem reads, "How the flowers of the aspen-plum flutter and turn! Do I not think of you? But your house is far away." The Master said, "Your thoughts were not really with him, or how could he be far away?"

BOOK X XIANG DANG

10. 1 Confucius, in his village, looked gentle and sincere, as if he were not able to speak. In the ancestorial temple or at court, he spoke readily but cautiously.

10. 2 At court when speaking with the officers of low rank, he looked affable and pleasant; when speaking with the officers of high rank, he looked upright and respectful. When the prince was present, his manner displayed respectful uneasiness; it was grave, but self-possessed.

10. 3 When the prince summoned him to receive guests, his countenance was solemn, his steps were swift. He bowed

【譯文】國君召孔子去接待外國的貴賓，他面色矜持莊重，腳步也快起來。向兩旁的人作揖，或者向左拱手，或者向右拱手，衣裳一俯一仰，都很整齊。快步向前，好像鳥兒舒展了翅膀。貴賓辭別以後，一定向國君報告說："客人已經不回頭了。"

10·4 入公門，鞠躬如也，如不容。

立不中門，行不履閾。

過位，色勃如也，足躩如也，其言似不足者。

攝齊升堂，鞠躬如也，屏氣似不息者。

出，降一等，逞顏色，怡怡如也。

没階，趨進，翼如也。

復其位，踧踖如也。

【譯文】孔子走進朝廷的門，謹慎而恭敬的樣子，好像没有容身之地。

不站在門的中間，行走不踩門坎。

經過國君的空座位，面色便矜持莊重，腳步也快起來，說話好像中氣不足似的。

提起下襬上堂，彎腰顯出恭敬謹慎的樣子，憋着氣，好像是不呼吸似的。

走出來，下一級臺階，面色便放鬆起來，怡然自得的樣子。

走完了階級，快步向前，好像鳥兒舒展了翅膀。

回到自己的席位，顯出恭敬而不安的樣子。

10·5 執圭，鞠躬如也，如不勝。上如揖，下如授。勃如戰色，足蹜蹜如有循。

享禮，有容色。

私覿，愉愉如也。

【譯文】孔子出使外國，會見國君，拿着圭，恭敬謹慎的樣子，

left and right to those beside him, straightened his robes in front and behind, and hastened forward, with his arms spreading like wings of a bird. When the guest had left, he would report to the prince, "The guest is no longer looking back."

10.4 Entering the palace gate he looked cautious and respectful, as if there were no room for him.

He did not stand in the middle of the gate, nor tread on the threshold.

Passing the throne, his countenance was solemn, his steps became swift, and his words came out as if he hardly had breath to utter them.

Ascending the dais, he held up his robe, bowed his back and held in his breath, as if he dared not breathe.

Coming down, after descending the first step, his countenance relaxed and bore a pleased look.

From the foot of the steps he advanced rapidly, with his arms spreading like wings of a bird.

When again in his seat his manner still showed respectful uneasiness.

10.5 When on an official mission to another state, the Master carried Gui①. He was respectful and cautious as if he were not able to lift it. He raised it as if he were making a bow. He lowered it as though he were making a presentation. He wore an awed look and dragged his feet, as though he were

---

① Symbol of the ruler's feudal investiture.

好像舉不起來,向上舉,好像在作揖;向下拿,好像在交給别人。面色戰戰兢兢,脚步也緊湊細小,好像沿着一條狹窄的路走過。

舉行獻禮物的禮儀時,滿臉和氣。

以私人身分會見外國君主,顯得很愉快。

10·6 君子不以紺緅飾,紅紫不以爲褻服。

當暑,袗絺綌,必表而出之。

緇衣,羔裘;素衣,麑裘;黄衣,狐裘。

褻裘長,短右袂。

必有寢衣,長一身有半。

狐貉之厚以居。

去喪,無所不佩。

非帷裳,必殺之。

羔裘玄冠不以弔。

吉月,必朝服而朝。

【譯文】君子不用天青色和鐵灰色的料子作鑲邊,淺紅色和紫色的料子不用來作平常在家穿的衣服。

在暑天,穿着粗的或者細的葛布單衣,但一定套在外面。

黑色的外衣配紫羔,白色的外衣配麑裘,黄色的外衣配狐裘。

平時在家的皮襖較長,右邊的袖子短一些。

睡覺一定有小被,有一個半人身長。

用狐、貉皮的厚毛做坐墊。

服喪滿了以後,什么東西都可以佩戴。

不是朝服和祭服,一定要剪裁。

紫羔和黑色禮帽,都不穿戴着去弔喪。

大年初一,一定穿着上朝的禮服去朝賀。

walking along a line.

When presenting ritual-gifts, he wore a placid appearance.

At the private audience, he looked cheerful.

10. 6 The superior man did not use purple or mauve in facings of his dress, nor did he use red or violet in his undress.

In hot weather he wore unlined linen clothes, but always over other garments.

Over lamb-skin he wore black; over fawn's fur he wore white, over fox-skin he wore yellow.

At home he wore a long fur robe, with the right sleeve short.

When sleeping he always had his quilt, which was half as long as his body.

The thick furs of the fox or badger were for cushions.

When out of mourning, he wore all his girdle-ornaments.

Except for court or sacrificial dress, his clothes must be cut.

He did not wear lamb's fur or a black cap on a visit of condolence.

On the first day of the year, he always went to court in full court dress.

10·7 齊,必有明衣,布。

齊必變食,居必遷坐。

【譯文】齋戒沐浴的時候,一定要有浴衣,用麻布做的。

齋戒的時候,一定改變平常的飲食,居住也一定搬移地方。

10·8 食不厭精,膾不厭細。

食饐而餲,魚餒而肉敗,不食。色惡,不食。臭惡,不食。失飪,不食。不時,不食。割不正,不食。不得其醬,不食。

肉雖多,不使勝食氣。

唯酒無量,不及亂。

沽酒市脯不食。

不撤薑食,不多食。

【譯文】糧食不嫌舂得精,魚和肉不嫌切得細。

飯食霉爛發臭,魚和肉腐爛,都不吃。食物顔色難看,不吃。氣味難聞,不吃。烹調不當,不吃。不到該吃時候,不吃。不是按一定方法宰割的肉,不吃。没有調味的醬醋,不吃。

席上肉雖然很多,吃肉不超過主食。

只有酒不限量,卻不至於喝醉。

買來的酒和肉乾不吃。

吃完了,薑不撤除,但吃得不多。

10·9 祭於公,不宿肉。祭肉不出三日。出三日,不食之矣。

【譯文】參與國家的祭祀典禮,不把分到的祭肉留到第二天。别的祭肉留存不超過三天。若是存放過了三天,便不吃它了。

10·10 食不語,寢不言。

10.7 On fast days he always wore a bathrobe made of linen cloth, changed his food and moved from the place where he commonly slept.

10.8 He did not dislike to have his rice finely cleaned, nor to have his meat finely minced.

He did not eat sour or mouldy rice, putrid fish, or tainted meat. Anything discoloured, or of a bad smell or badly cooked, he would not eat. He did not eat when it was not the right time for meals. He did not eat meat which was not properly cut, nor a dish without its proper sauce.

Though there was lots of meat, he would not eat more meat than rice.

To wine alone he set no limit, but he did not drink till he was inebriated.

He did not drink bought wine, or eat ready-dried market meat.

After the meal, ginger was not taken away, But he did not eat much.

10.9 After sacrifice at the palace, he would not keep the meat which he received over night. The meat of other sacrifice he did not keep over three days. If kept longer it was not eaten.

10.10 He did not talk at meals, nor speak when in bed.

【譯文】吃飯的時候不交談，睡覺的時候不說話。

10·11　雖疏食菜羹，必祭，必齊如也。

【譯文】即使吃的是粗米飯、菜湯，臨吃前也要先祭一祭，而且表情嚴肅恭敬。

10·12　席不正，不坐。

【譯文】坐席不端正，不坐。

10·13　鄉人飲酒，杖者出，斯出矣。

【譯文】同本鄉人喝酒，等老年人都散去了，自己才出去。

10·14　鄉人儺，朝服而立於阼階。

【譯文】本地方的人迎神驅鬼，便穿着朝服站在東邊的臺階上。

10·15　問人於他邦，再拜而送之。

【譯文】託人向外國的朋友問好送禮，便向受托者拜兩次後送行。

10·16　康子饋藥，拜而受之。曰："丘未達，不敢嘗。"

【譯文】季康子給孔子送藥，孔子作揖行禮後接受了。說："我對藥性不瞭解，不敢試服。"

10·17　廄焚。子退朝，曰："傷人乎？"不問馬。

【譯文】馬棚失火。孔子從朝廷回來，說："傷了人嗎？"沒問到馬。

10. 11 Although his food was coarse rice and vegetable soup, he still would offer a little of it in sacrifice with a grave respectful air.

10. 12 If his mat was not straight he did not sit on it.

10. 13 When drinking with the villagers, he left the feast only after the elders had gone out.

10. 14 At the village exorcisms he put on his court dress and stood on the eastern steps.

10. 15 When sending inquires to his friends in another state, he bowed twice and saw his messenger off.

10. 16 When Ji Kang Zi sent him some medicine, he bowed and received it, saying, "I do not know it, I dare not taste it."

10. 17 His stables having been burnt, Confucius, on his return from the court, said, "Is anyone hurt?" He did not ask about horses.

10·18 君賜食,必正席先嘗之。君賜腥,必熟而薦之。君賜生,必畜之。

侍食於君,君祭,先飯。

【譯文】國君賜給食品,一定擺正坐位先嘗一嘗。國君賜給生肉,一定煮熟了,先供奉祖先。國君賜給活物,一定畜養着。

侍奉國君吃飯,當國君舉行飯前祭禮的時候,自己先吃飯。

10·19 疾,君視之,東首,加朝服,拖紳。

【譯文】孔子病了,國君來探問,他頭朝東,把上朝的禮服蓋在身上,拖着大帶。

10·20 君命召,不俟駕行矣。

【譯文】國君召喚,孔子便不等待車輛駕好馬,立即動身。

10·21 入太廟,每事問。

【譯文】孔子到了周公廟,每件事都要詢問。

10·22 朋友死,無所歸,曰:"於我殯。"

【譯文】朋友死了,没有料理的人,孔子說:"喪葬由我來料理。"

10·23 朋友之饋,雖車馬,非祭肉,不拜。

【譯文】朋友的饋贈,即使是車馬,只要不是祭肉,不行禮。

10·24 寢不尸,居不客。

【譯文】孔子睡覺不像死屍一樣仰天直躺,平日坐着,也不像

10. 18 When the prince sent him a present of food, he must set his mat straight, and taste it first. When the prince sent him raw meat, he must cook it and make a sacrificial offering. When the prince sent him a living beast, he must rear it.

When dining in attendance on the prince, the prince made the sacrificial offering, he ate first.

10. 19 When he was sick and the prince came to see him, he had his head to the east and had his court dress spread across him, with the girdle over it.

10. 20 When summoned by the prince, he went at once without waiting for his carriage to be yoked.

10. 21 When he entered the Grand Temple, he asked about everything.

10. 22 When a friend died and nobody was in charge of his funeral, the Master said, "Leave the funeral to me."

10. 23 When a friend sent him a gift, though it might be a carriage and horses, so long as it was not sacrificial meat, he would not bow.

10. 24 When sleeping he did not lie like a corpse. At home he did not kneel on the mat as if receiving guests.

接見客人或者自己做客人一樣，兩膝跪在席上。

10·25 見齊衰者，雖狎，必變。見冕者與瞽者，雖褻，必以貌。

凶服者式之。式負版者。

有盛饌，必變色而作。

迅雷風烈必變。

【譯文】孔子看見穿齊衰孝服的人，就是極親密的，也一定變得嚴肅。看見戴着禮帽和瞎了眼睛的人，即使很熟悉，也一定有禮貌。

遇着拿了送死人衣物的人，便在車中把身體微微地向前一俯，手伏着車前的横木致禮。遇見背負國家圖籍的人，也手伏車前横木示禮。

有豐富的菜餚，一定改變神色，站立起來。

遇見迅雷、大風，一定改變神色。

10·26 升車，必正立，執綏。

車中，不内顧，不疾言，不親指。

【譯文】孔子上車，一定先端正地站着，抓着扶手帶登車。

在車中，不向内回顧，不很快地説話，不用手指指畫畫。

10·27 色斯舉矣，翔而後集。曰："山梁雌雉，時哉時哉！"子路共之，三嗅而作。

【譯文】野鷄見到顔色不善就飛了，盤旋飛翔了一陣又聚集停在一處。孔子説："山梁上的這些雌雉，得其時呀！得其時呀！"子路向它們拱了拱手，野鷄又拍拍翅膀飛走了。

10. 25 On seeing anyone in mourning, though he might be a friend, the Master would put on a solemn expression; on seeing anyone in full dress, or a blind man, though he knew him well, he would show a polite attitude to him.

When seeing a man in mourning from his carriage, he would bow forward to the cross-bar; he also bowed over the crossbar to the census-bearers.

Before a particularly choice dainty he would change countenance and rise up.

On a sudden clap of thunder, or a voilent gust of wind, he would change countenance.

10. 26 When mounting his carriage, he would stand straight and hold the cord.

When in the carriage, he did not look around, or speak hastily, or point with his hands.

10. 27 Seeing the countenance, the hen pheasants instantly rose, flew around and by and by settled. The Master said, "These hen pheasants on the hill-bridge! At their season! At their season!" Zilu made a motion to them. They spread their wings and flew away.

先進篇第十一

11·1 子曰："先進於禮樂，野人也；後進於禮樂，君子也。如用之，則吾從先進。"

【譯文】孔子說："先學習禮樂而後作官的，是普通讀書人；先有了官位而後學習禮樂的，是卿大夫世家子弟。如果我選用人才，我主張選用先學習禮樂的。"

11·2 子曰："從我於陳、蔡者，皆不及門也。"

【譯文】孔子說："跟着我在陳國、蔡國之間忍饑受餓的人，都不在我這裏了。"

11·3 德行：顔淵，閔子騫，冉伯牛，仲弓。言語：宰我，子貢。政事：冉有，季路。文學：子游，子夏。

【譯文】孔子的學生德行好的：顔淵，閔子騫，冉伯牛，仲弓。能言善辯的：宰我，子貢。善於辦理政事的：冉有，季路。熟悉古代文獻的：子游，子夏。

11·4 子曰："回也非助我者也，於吾言無所不説。"

【譯文】孔子說："顔回不是對我有所幫助的人，他對我的話沒有不喜歡的。"

11·5 子曰："孝哉閔子騫！人不間於其父母昆弟之言。"

【譯文】孔子說："閔子騫真是孝順呀！別人對於他父母兄弟稱贊他的話，從無異議。"

11·6 南容三復白圭，孔子以其兄之子妻之。

BOOK XI XIAN JIN

11. 1 The Master said, "Those who learned ritual and music first and then took office were the common people; those who took office first and then learned ritual and music were the sons of officials. If I were to appoint someone, I favored the one who learned ritual and music first."

11. 2 The Master said, "None of those who were with me in the states of Chen and Cai come any more to my door!"

11. 3 Distinguished for their virtue, there were Yan Yuan, Min Ziqian, Ran Boniu and Zhong Gong; for their ability in speech, Zai Wo and Zigong; for their administrative talents, Ran You and Ji Lu; for their literary acquirements, Ziyou and Zixia.

11. 4 The Master said, "I get no help from Hui. No words I say but delights him!"

11. 5 The Master said, "Filial indeed is Min Ziqian! Other people can say nothing of him different from the praises by his parents and brothers."

11. 6 Nan Rong was frequently repeating the lines in the

【譯文】南容把《詩經》中"白圭之玷,尚可磨也;斯言之玷,不可為也"這幾句詩讀了又讀,孔子把他哥哥的女兒嫁給他。

11·7 季康子問:"弟子孰爲好學?"孔子對曰:"有顔回者好學,不幸短命死矣,今也則亡。"

【譯文】季康子問道:"你學生中誰愛好學習?"孔子回答說:"有一個叫顏回的愛好學習,不幸短命死了,現在就沒有了。"

11·8 顔淵死,顔路請子之車以爲之椁。子曰:"才不才,亦各言其子也。鯉也死,有棺而無椁。吾不徒行以爲之椁。以吾從大夫之後,不可徒行也。"

【譯文】顏淵死了,他的父親顏路請求孔子賣掉車子來替顏淵做外椁。孔子說:"不管有才能還是沒有才能,也是各人自己的兒子。我的兒子鯉死了,只有內棺,沒有外椁。我不能賣掉車子步行來替他做外椁。因為我還跟隨在大夫之後,是不可以步行的。"

11·9 顔淵死。子曰:"噫!天喪予!天喪予!"

【譯文】顏淵死了,孔子說:"唉!上天要我的命呀!上天要我的命呀!"

11·10 顔淵死,子哭之慟。從者曰:"子慟矣!"曰:"有慟乎?非夫人之爲慟而誰爲?"

【譯文】顏淵死了,孔子哭得非常悲痛,跟隨孔子的人說:"您太悲哀了!"孔子說:"真的太悲哀了嗎?我不為這樣的人悲哀,還為什麼人傷心呢!"

11·11 顔淵死,門人欲厚葬之。子曰:"不可。"

Book of Poetry: "A flaw in a white sceptre-stone may be ground away, but for a flaw in speech, nothing can be done." Confucius married Nan Rong his elder brother's daughter.

11.7 Ji Kangzi asked which of his disciples loved learning. Confucius answered, "There was Hui. He loved learning. Unfortunately he was short-lived and died. Now there is no one."

11.8 When Yan Yuan died, his father Yan Lu asked for the Master's carriage to make an enclosure for his son's coffin. The Master said, "Whether gifted or not, each one speaks of his son. When my son Li died, he only had a coffin but no enclosure. I would not walk on foot to furnish an enclosure. Because, following after the great officers, it was not proper for me to walk on foot."

11.9 When Yan Yuan died, the Master said, "Alas! Heaven is destroying me! Heaven is destroying me!"

11.10 When Yan Yuan died the Master gave way to grief. Those with him said, "Sir, your grief is excessive." The Master said, "Is it excessive? If for this man I did not give way to grief, for whom should I give way?"

11.11 When Yan Yuan died the disciples wished to give

門人厚葬之。子曰:“回也視予猶父也,予不得視猶子也。非我也,夫二三子也。”

【譯文】顔淵死了,孔子的學生們想要厚葬他。孔子說:“不可以。”

學生們仍然厚葬了他。孔子說:“顔回看待我好像父親一樣,我卻不能夠像對待兒子一樣看待你。這不是我的主意呀,是你那幫同學幹的呀。”

11·12 季路問事鬼神。子曰:“未能事人,焉能事鬼?”

曰:“敢問死。”曰:“未知生,焉知死?”

【譯文】子路問怎樣事奉鬼神。孔子說:“還没能服事活人,怎麽能去服事鬼呢?”

子路又説:“我大膽地請問死是怎麽回事。”孔子說:“還没有弄明白生,怎麽能夠懂得死?”

11·13 閔子侍側,誾誾如也;子路,行行如也;冉有、子貢,侃侃如也。子樂。“若由也,不得其死然。”

【譯文】閔子騫站在孔子身旁,恭敬而正直的樣子;子路很剛强的樣子;冉有、子貢溫和而快樂的樣子。孔子高興了。但又說:“像仲由吧,怕得不到好死。”

11·14 魯人爲長府。閔子騫曰:“仍舊貫,如之何?何必改作?”子曰:“夫人不言,言必有中。”

【譯文】魯國翻修叫長府的金庫。閔子騫說:“依舊照着老樣子,怎麽樣?為什麽一定要翻修呢?”孔子說:“這個人平日不說話,一開口一定說得正確。”

11·15 子曰:“由之瑟奚爲於丘之門?”門人不敬子路。子

him a great funeral, and the Master said, "You cannot do so."

The disciples did bury him in great style. The Master said, "Hui treated me as a father; I have failed to treat him as a son. No, it was not my idea. It was your doing, my disciples!"

11. 12 Jilu asked about serving the spirits of the dead. The Master said, "While you are not able to serve the living, how can you serve their spirits?"

Jilu added, "I venture to ask about death." The Master said, "While you do not know life, how can you know about death?"

11. 13 Standing by the side of the Master, Min Ziqian looked respectful and honest; Zilu looked bold and soldierly; Ran You and Zigong looked genial and pleasant. The Master was pleased. But he said, "A man like Zhong You, will not die a natural death."

11. 14 The Men of Lu were rebuilding the treasury of Changfu, Min Ziqian said, "Would not the old one do? Why must a new one be built?" The Master said, "That man seldom speaks; when he does, he is sure to hit the point."

11. 15 The Master said, "Why does Zhong You play Se[①]

① A large horizontal musical instrument.

曰:“由也升堂矣,未入於室也。”

【譯文】孔子說:“仲由彈瑟為什麼在我這裏來彈奏呢?”孔子的學生們因此不尊敬子路。孔子說:“仲由在學問上已經是升堂了,只是還沒入室罷了。”

11·16 子貢問:“師與商也孰賢?”子曰:“師也過,商也不及。”

曰:“然則師愈與?”子曰:“過猶不及。”

【譯文】子貢問孔子:“顓孫師和卜商,誰好一些?”孔子說:“顓孫師有些過分,卜商有些趕不上。”

子貢說:“那麼,顓孫師好一些嗎?”孔子說:“過分和趕不上同樣不好。”

11·17 季氏富於周公,而求也爲之聚斂而附益之。子曰:“非吾徒也。小子鳴鼓而攻之,可也。”

【譯文】季氏比周公還富足,冉求又替他搜括,增加更多的財富。孔子說:“冉求不是我的學生,你們學生可以大張旗鼓地攻擊他。”

11·18 柴也愚,參也魯,師也辟,由也喭。

【譯文】高柴愚笨,曾參遲鈍,顓孫師偏激,仲由鹵莽。

11·19 子曰:“回也其庶乎,屢空。賜不受命,而貨殖焉,億則屢中。”

【譯文】孔子說:“顏回的學問道德差不多了吧,可是常常窮得什麼也沒有。端木賜不聽天由命,去囤積投機,猜測行情,竟每每猜對了。”

in my house?"Whereupon the other disciples began not to respect Zilu. The Master said, "In learning Zhong You has ascended to the hall, but he has not yet entered the inner rooms."

11. 16 Zigong asked, "Who is the better, Shi [①] or Shang [②]?" The Master said, "Shi goes too far; Shang goes not far enough."

Zigong said, "Then Shi is the better, I suppose." The Master said, "Too far is no better than not far enough."

11. 17 The head of the Ji family was richer than the Duke of Zhou, and yet Ran Qiu collected taxes for him and increased his wealth. The Master said, "He is no disciple of mine. My disciples, beat the drum and assail him."

11. 18 Chai [③] is stupid, Shen is dull, Shi is extreme, Zhong You is rash.

11. 19 The Master said, "Hui has nearly attained perfect virtue, but he is often in want. Ci does not bow to fate. He engages in speculation and cornering. In his calculations he often hits the mark."

---

① i. e. Zizhang.

② i. e. Zixia.

③ Gao Chai, disciple of Confucius.

11·20　子張問善人之道。子曰："不踐迹，亦不入於室。"

【譯文】子張問怎樣做個善人。孔子說："善人不踩着別人的腳印走，但是，學問道德也難以長進到家。"

11·21　子曰："論篤是與，君子者乎？色莊者乎？"

【譯文】孔子說："人們總是贊揚說話誠實的人，但這種人是真正的君子呢？還是神情外表莊重的人呢？"

11·22　子路問："聞斯行諸？"子曰："有父兄在，如之何其聞斯行之？"

冉有問："聞斯行諸？"子曰："聞斯行之。"

公西華曰："由也問聞斯行諸，子曰，'有父兄在'；求也問聞斯行諸，子曰，'聞斯行之'。赤也惑，敢問。"子曰："求也退，故進之；由也兼人，故退之。"

【譯文】子路問："聽到就幹起來嗎？"孔子說："有父親和兄長活着，怎麼能聽到就幹起來？"

冉有問："聽到就幹起來嗎？"孔子說："聽到就幹起來。"

公西華說："仲由問聽到就幹起來嗎，您說'有父親和兄長活着'，冉求問聽到就幹起來嗎，您說'聽到就幹起來'。我有些糊塗，大膽地請問這是為什麼。"孔子說："冉求平日做事退縮，所以我向前推動他，仲由的膽量有兩個人的大，所以我要讓他向後退縮。"

11·23　子畏於匡，顏淵後。子曰："吾以女爲死矣。"曰："子在，回何敢死？"

【譯文】孔子在匡地被囚禁，顏淵最後才來。孔子說："我以為你死了。"顏淵說："您還活着，我怎麼敢死呢？"

11. 20 Zizhang asked what was the way of a good man. The Master said, "He does not tread in the footsteps of others, nor do his virtue and learning attain to perfection."

11. 21 The Master said, "People always approve of a man whose discourse seems solid and sincere. But is he really a superior man, or one who merely adopts outward airs of solemnity?"

11. 22 Zilu asked, "Shall I immediately put into practice what I heard?" The Master said, "While your father and elder brother are alive, how can you immediately put what you heard into practice?"

Ran You asked, "Shall I immediately put into practice what I heard?" The Master said, "Immediately put into practice what you heard."

Gongxi Hua said, "Zhong You asked whether he should do immediately what he heard and you said, 'While your father and elder brothers are alive.' Qiu asked whether he should do immediately what he heard, and you said, 'Immediately put into practice what you heard.' I am confused, and venture to ask you." The Master said, "Qiu is bashful, so I egged him on; Zhong You has the plack of two, so I held him back."

11. 23 The Master was trapped in Kuang and Yan Hui fell behind. The Master said, "I thought you had died." Hui replied, "While you are alive, how shall I dare to die?"

11·24 季子然問："仲由、冉求可謂大臣與？"子曰："吾以子爲異之問，曾由與求之問。所謂大臣者，以道事君，不可則止。今由與求也，可謂具臣矣。"

曰："然則從之者與？"子曰："弑父與君，亦不從也。"

【譯文】季子然問："仲由和冉求可以說是大臣嗎？"孔子説："我以為你是問别的人，竟只是問仲由和冉求。我們所説的大臣，是用正確的原則來事奉君主，行不通，就不幹。如今仲由和冉求，可以説是具有相當才能的臣屬了。"

季子然又説："那麼，他們會一切都順從上級嗎？"孔子説："殺父親、殺君主的事情，他們也不會順從的。"

11·25 子路使子羔爲費宰。子曰："賊夫人之子。"

子路曰："有民人焉，有社稷焉，何必讀書，然後爲學？"

子曰："是故惡夫佞者。"

【譯文】子路派子羔去做費縣縣長。孔子説："這是害了這個年輕人了。"

子路説："那地方有老百姓，有土地和五谷，為什麼一定要讀書才叫做學習呢？"

孔子説："所以我討厭尖嘴利舌的人。"

11·26 子路、曾晳、冉有、公西華侍坐。

子曰："以吾一日長乎爾，毋吾以也。居則曰：'不吾知也！'如或知爾，則何以哉？"

子路率爾而對曰："千乘之國，攝乎大國之間，加之以師旅，因之以饑饉，由也爲之，比及三年，可使有勇，且知方也。"

夫子哂之。

"求，爾何如？"

對曰："方六七十，如五六十，求也爲之，比及三年，可使足

11.24 Ji Ziran asked whether Zhong You and Ran Qiu could be called great ministers. The Master said, "I thought you would ask about somebody else, and you ask only about Zhong You and Qiu! What is called a great minister, is one who serves his prince according to what is right, and when he finds he cannot do so, retires. Now, as for Zhong You and Qiu, they may be called ordinary ministers."

Ji Ziran said, "Then they will always follow their chief, will they?" The Master said, "In an act of slaying their prince or their father, they would not follow him."

11.25 Zilu made Zigao[①] governor of Fei. The Master said, "You are doing harm to this young man."

Zilu said, "There are the people, there are the altars of the spirits of the land and grain there: why only reading can be called learning?" The Master said, "This is why I hate glib-tongued people."

11.26 Zilu, Zeng Xi[②], Ran You, and Gongxi Hua were sitting by the Master.

The Master said, "I may be older than you, but do not think of that. You often say, 'We are not known.' Well, if some prince were to know you, what would you do?"

---

① i.e. Gao Chai.

② The father of Zeng Zi, disciple of Confucius.

民。如其禮樂，以俟君子。”

“赤，爾何如？”

對曰：“非曰能之，願學焉。宗廟之事，如會同，端章甫，願爲小相焉。”

“點，爾何如？”

鼓瑟希，鏗爾，舍瑟而作，對曰：“異乎三子者之撰。”

子曰：“何傷乎？亦各言其志也。”

曰：“莫春者，春服既成，冠者五六人，童子六七人，浴乎沂，風乎舞雩，詠而歸。”

夫子喟然歎曰：“吾與點也！”

三子者出，曾晳後。曾晳曰：“夫三子者之言何如？”

子曰：“亦各言其志也已矣。”

曰：“夫子何哂由也？”

曰：“爲國以禮，其言不讓，是故哂之。”

“唯求則非邦也與？”

“安見方六七十如五六十而非邦也者？”

“唯赤則非邦也與？”

“宗廟會同，非諸侯而何？赤也爲之小，孰能爲之大？”

【譯文】子路、曾晳、冉有、公西華四個人陪着孔子坐着。

孔子說：“因為我比你們年紀都大一些，（老了，）不要因為我年長而不敢說。你們平常說：‘人家不知道我呀！’假如有人瞭解你們，那你們怎麽辦呢？”

子路急忙輕率地回答：“一千輛兵車的國家，在大國之間受逼迫，外面有軍隊侵犯它，加上國內又鬧災荒。我去治理，等到三年，可使人人有勇氣，而且懂得禮義。”

孔子微微一笑。

又問：“冉求，你怎麽樣？”

冉求回答說：“國土縱横各六七十里或者五六十里的小國

Zilu hastily and lightly answered, "Give me charge of a state of a thousand chariots, hemmed in by powerful neighbours, invaded by foreign armies, and searched by famine at home, in three years' time I could make the people to be bold, and to recognize the rules of righteous conduct."

The Master smiled.

"What would you do, Qiu?" he asked.

Qiu answered, "Had I charge a state of sixty or seventy square miles, or one of fifty or sixty, in three years' time I could give the people plenty. As to teaching ritual and music, I would wait for the rise of a superior man to do that."

"And what would you do, Chi?"

Chi answered, "I speak of the things I would like to learn, not of what I can do. At service in the ancestral temple, or at the audience of the princes, I would like, in full dress, to act as a small assistant."

"And what would you do, Dian①?"

Dian ceased to play, pushed his still sounding Se aside, rose and answered, "My wishes are different from those of the other three."

The Master said, "What harm in that? Each but speak his mind."

Zeng Xi said, "In the last days of spring, with the dress of

---

① i. e. Zeng Xi.

家,我去治理,等到三年,可使人民富足。至於禮樂教化,那只有等待賢人君子了。"

又問:"公西赤,你怎麽樣?"

公西赤回答説:"不是説我有本領,但我願意學習。在宗廟舉行祭祀,或者同外國盟會,我願意穿着禮服,戴着禮帽,做一個小司儀。"

又問:"曾點,你怎麽樣?"

他彈瑟接近尾聲,鏗的一聲把瑟放下,站了起來,回答説:"我的志向和他們三位所講的不同。"

孔子説:"那有什麽關系呢?只是各人説説自己的志向罷了!"

曾皙便説:"暮春三月,春天衣服都穿上了,我陪同五六位成年人,六七個小孩,在沂水旁邊洗洗澡,在舞雩臺上吹吹風,一路唱着歌走回來。"

孔子長嘆一聲説:"我同意曾點的想法啊!"

子路、冉有、公西華三人都退了出去,曾皙走在後面。曾皙説:"那三位的話怎麽樣?"

孔子説:"也不過各人説説自己的志向罷了。"

曾皙又説:"您為什麽笑仲由呢?"

孔子説:"治理國家應該講求禮讓,可是他的話卻一點不謙虚,所以笑他。"

"難道冉求所講的就不是國家嗎?"

孔子説:"怎見得縱横各六七十里或者五六十里的土地就不是一個國家呢?"

"公西赤所講的不是國家嗎?"

孔子説:"有宗廟,有國際間的盟會,不是國家是什麽?公西赤如果他只能做一個小司儀者,誰能夠做大司儀者呢?"

the season all complete, along with five or six young men and six or seven boys, I would bathe in the Yi River, enjoy the breeze at Wuyu (the Rain Dance altar), and return home singing."

The Master sighed and said, "I am with Dian."

The three others having gone out, Zeng Xi remained behind, and said, "What do you think of what the others said?"

"Each but speak his mind," said the Master.

"Why did you smile at Zhong You?"

"The management of a state demands the rules of propriety, but what he said was not modest. That was why I smiled at him."

"But did not Qiu speak of a state?"

"Did you ever see a territory of sixty or seventy Le, or one of fifty or sixty, which was not a state?"

"And did not Chi, too, speak of a state?"

"Who but princes would there be in the Ancestral Temple, or at the Grand Audience? If Chi were to be a small assistant in these services, who could be a great one?"

顏淵篇第十二

12·1 顏淵問仁。子曰:"克己復禮爲仁。一日克己復禮,天下歸仁焉。爲仁由己,而由人乎哉?"

顏淵曰:"請問其目。"子曰:"非禮勿視,非禮勿聽,非禮勿言,非禮勿動。"

顏淵曰:"回雖不敏,請事斯語矣。"

【譯文】顏淵問什麼是仁。孔子說:"克制自己,使言語行動都合於禮,就是仁。一旦這樣做到了,天下的人都會稱許你是仁人。實踐仁德,全靠自己,還靠別人嗎?"

顏淵說:"請問實行仁德的具體條目。"孔子說:"不合禮的不看,不合禮的不聽,不合禮的不說,不合禮的不做。"

顏淵說:"我雖然遲鈍,也要按照您這些話去實行。"

12·2 仲弓問仁。子曰:"出門如見大賓,使民如承大祭。己所不欲,勿施於人。在邦無怨,在家無怨。"

仲弓曰:"雍雖不敏,請事斯語矣。"

【譯文】仲弓問什麼是仁。孔子說:"出門工作好像去接待貴賓,役使百姓好像去承當大的祀典。自己不喜歡的,不強加給別人。在工作職位上無所怨恨,不在工作職位上也無所怨恨。"

仲弓說:"我雖然不聰敏,也要照您這話去做。"

12·3 司馬牛問仁。子曰:"仁者,其言也訒。"

曰:"其言也訒,斯謂之仁已乎?"子曰:"爲之難,言之得無訒乎?"

【譯文】司馬牛問什麼是仁。孔子說:"仁人,他的言語遲鈍。"

司馬牛說:"言語遲鈍,這就叫做仁了嗎?"孔子說:"做起來

BOOK XII YAN YUAN

12. 1 Yan Yuan asked about perfect virtue. The Master said, "To subdue one's-self and turn to propriety is perfect virtue. If a man can subdue himself and turn to propriety, everyone under heaven would praise him as a man of perfect virtue. The practice of perfect virtue is from a man himself, is it from others?"

Yan Yuan said, "May I ask for the more detailed items of this?" The Master said, "Do not look at what is contrary to propriety; do not listen to what is contrary to propriety; do not speak what is contrary to propriety; do not do what is contrary to propriety."

Yan Yuan then said, "Though I am dull, I hope to live by these words."

12. 2 Zhonggong asked about perfect virtue. The Master said, "When away from home, to behave as though you were receiving a great guest; to employ the people as though you were assisting at a great sacrifice; do not do to others what you do not wish yourself; do not bear resentment either in the state or in the family."

Zhonggong said, "Though I am dull, I hope to live by these words."

12. 3 Sima Niu asked about perfect virtue. The Master said, "The man of perfect virtue is cautious and slow in his speech."

"Cautious and slow in his speech!" said Niu, "is this what

很難，說起來能夠不遲鈍嗎？"

12·4 司馬牛問君子。子曰："君子不憂不懼。"

曰："不憂不懼，斯謂之君子已乎？"子曰："內省不疚，夫何憂何懼？"

【譯文】司馬牛問怎樣做一個君子。孔子說："君子不憂愁，不恐懼。"

司馬牛說："不憂愁，不恐懼，這就叫做君子了嗎？"孔子說："內心反省自己毫不愧疚，有什麼可憂愁，可害怕的呢？"

12·5 司馬牛憂曰："人皆有兄弟，我獨亡。"子夏曰："商聞之矣：死生有命，富貴在天。君子敬而無失，與人恭而有禮。四海之內，皆兄弟也。君子何患乎無兄弟也？"

【譯文】司馬牛憂愁地說："別人都有兄弟，單單我沒有。"子夏道："我聽說過：死生聽之命運，富貴由天安排。君子只是對待工作嚴肅認真，不出差錯，對待別人恭謹，合乎禮節，天下到處都是兄弟，君子又何必擔憂沒有兄弟呢？"

12·6 子張問明。子曰："浸潤之譖，膚受之愬，不行焉，可謂明也已矣。浸潤之譖，膚受之愬，不行焉，可謂遠也已矣。"

【譯文】子張問什麼是明智。孔子說："點滴而來、日積月累的讒言和肌膚所受、切身之痛的誣告，在你這裏行不通，那你可以說是明智了。點滴而來、日積月累的讒言和肌膚所受、切身之痛的誣告，在你這裏行不通，可以說是有遠見的了。"

12·7 子貢問政。子曰："足食，足兵，民信之矣。"

子貢曰："必不得已而去，於斯三者何先？"曰："去兵。"

子貢曰："必不得已而去，於斯二者何先？"曰："去食。自古皆

is meant by perfect virtue?"The Master said,"That which is hard to do,can it be lightly spoken?"

12.4 Sima Niu asked what is a superior man. The Master said,"A superior man has neither anxiety nor fear."

"No anxiety and no fear!"said Niu,"Does this constitute what we call a superior man?"The Master said,"When internal examination finds nothing wrong,what should he be anxious about?What should he fear?"

12.5 Sima Niu said sadly,"All men have brothers,I alone have none!"Zixia said,"I have heard that life and death are determined by fate,that wealth and honours depend upon the will of Heaven. A superior man attends to business carefully and does not trip;he is respectful to others and observant of propriety. All within the world will be his brothers. How can a superior man feel distressed about his lack of them?"

12.6 Zizhang asked what constituted intelligence. The Master said,"He who is influenced neither by slander that gradually soaks into the mind,nor by calumny that startles like a wound in the flesh,may be called intelligent indeed. Yes,he is influenced neither by soaking slander nor by startling calumny may be called far-sighted."

12.7 Zigong asked about government. The Master said,"Sufficient food,sufficient military equipment,and the confidence of the people in their ruler."

有死，民無信不立。”

【譯文】子貢問怎樣治理國家。孔子說：“糧食充足，軍備充足，民衆對政府便信賴了。”

子貢說：“如果迫不得已在糧食、軍備、民衆信賴三項之中要去掉一項，先去掉哪一項？”孔子說：“不要軍備。”

子貢說：“如果迫不得已，在糧食和人民信賴兩者之中要去掉一項，去掉哪一項呢？”孔子說：“不要糧食。自古以來，誰都免不了一死，失去人民的信賴，政府便站不住腳了。”

12·8 棘子成曰：“君子質而已矣，何以文爲？”子貢曰：“惜乎，夫子之說君子也！駟不及舌。文猶質也，質猶文也。虎豹之鞟猶犬羊之鞟。”

【譯文】棘子成說：“君子只要本質好就行了，要什麼文彩呢？”子貢說：“遺憾啊，先生這樣談論君子！一言既出，駟馬難追。文彩如同本質，本質也如同文彩，二者是同樣重要的。把虎豹和犬羊身上有文彩的毛都拔去，它們的皮革就一樣了。”

12·9 哀公問於有若曰：“年饑，用不足，如之何？”

有若對曰：“盍徹乎？”

曰：“二，吾猶不足，如之何其徹也？”

對曰：“百姓足，君孰與不足？百姓不足，君孰與足？”

【譯文】魯哀公問有若說：“年成欠收，國家費用不夠，怎麼辦？”

有若回答說：“何不實行十分抽一的稅率呢？”

魯哀公說：“十分抽二我都不夠，怎麼能十分抽一呢？”

有若回答說：“如果百姓費用夠，您怎麼會不夠？如果百姓費用不夠，您怎麼會夠？”

Zigong said, "If it cannot be helped, and one of these three must be dispensed with, which should be forgone first?" "The military equipment," said the Master.

Zigong asked, "If it cannot be helped, and one of the remaining two must be dispensed with, which should be forgone?" The Master said, "Food. From of old, death has been the lot of all men; but if the people have no confidence in their ruler, a state cannot stand."

12.8 Ji Zicheng said, "Only the substantial qualities are wanted in a superior man. What can ornamental accomplishments do for him?" The Master said, "I'm sorry, sir, that you spoke of a superior man in such a way. Even a team of four horses cannot overtake and recover what is already said. Ornament is as substance; substance is as ornament. Without the fur, a tiger or a leopard's hide is like the hide of a dog, or goat."

12.9 Duke Ai said to You Rou, "In this year of dearth, the state has not enough for needs; what should be done?"

You Rou answered, "Why not levy a one-tenth tax on people?"

"With two tenths," said the duke, "I find them not enough, how could the system of one tenth avail?"

You Rou said, "When the people all live in plenty, will the prince alone be in want? If the people are all in want, can the prince alone live in plenty?"

12·10 子張問崇德辨惑。子曰:"主忠信,徙義,崇德也。愛之欲其生,惡之欲其死。既欲其生,又欲其死,是惑也。'誠不以富,亦衹以異。'"

【譯文】子張問怎麽樣提高品德,釋疑辨惑,孔子說:"以忠誠信實爲主,凡事按情理去幹,這就能提高品德。喜愛一個人,希望他長命百歲,厭惡一個人,便恨不得他立刻死去。既要他長壽,又要他死去,這便是迷惑。'這樣,對自己毫無好處,只是使人家奇怪罷了。'"

12·11 齊景公問政於孔子。孔子對曰:"君君,臣臣,父父,子子。"公曰:"善哉!信如君不君,臣不臣,父不父,子不子,雖有粟,吾得而食諸?"

【譯文】齊景公問孔子怎樣治理國家。孔子回答說:"國君要像個國君,臣子要像個臣子,父親要像個父親,兒子要像個兒子。"齊景公說:"好呀!假若國君真不像個國君,臣子真不像個臣子,父親真不像個父親,兒子真不像個兒子,即便有糧食,我能夠吃得着嗎?"

12·12 子曰:"片言可以折獄者,其由也與?"

子路無宿諾。

【譯文】孔子說:"根據單方面的話,就可以判決訴訟案件的,恐怕只有仲由吧?"

子路從不拖延履行諾言。

12·13 子曰:"聽訟,吾猶人也。必也使無訟乎!"

【譯文】孔子說:"審理訴訟,我和别人差不多。但一定要使訴訟案件没有才好。"

12. 10 Zizhang asked how to exalt virtue and scatter delusion. The Master said, "Hold faithfulness and sincerity as first principles, and follow righteousness; your virtue will be exalted. You love a man and wish him to live; you hate him, and wish him to die. To wish him both life and death is a case of delusion. 'It was no help to himself, but only made others confused.'"

12. 11 Duke Jing of Qi asked Confucius about government. Confucius said, "Let the ruler be ruler, the minister minister, the father father, and the son son." "True indeed!" said the duke, "If the ruler is not ruler, the minister not minister, the father not father, and the son not son, although the abundant grain was there, could I get enough to eat?"

12. 12 The Master siad, "It is only Zhong You who could settle lawsuits on hearing one-sideded words!"

Zilu never slept over a promise.

12. 13 The Master said, "At hearing lawsuits I am like anybody else. What is necessary is to cause the people to have no lawsuits."

12·14 子張問政。子曰:“居之無倦,行之以忠。”

【譯文】子張問怎樣作官。孔子説:“在職位上不疲沓偷懶,辦起公事忠實盡力。”

12·15 子曰:“博學於文,約之以禮,亦可以弗畔矣夫!”

【譯文】孔子説:“君子廣泛地學習文獻,再用禮節來約束,也就可以不致于離經叛道了。”

12·16 子曰:“君子成人之美,不成人之惡。小人反是。”

【譯文】孔子説:“君子成全别人的好事,不促成别人的壞事。小人和這相反。”

12·17 季康子問政於孔子。孔子對曰:“政者,正也。子帥以正,孰敢不正?”

【譯文】季康子向孔子問什麽是政治。孔子説:“政治的意思是端正。您帶頭端正行為,誰敢不端正呢?”

12·18 季康子患盜,問於孔子。孔子對曰:“苟子之不欲,雖賞之不竊。”

【譯文】季康子苦於盜賊太多,向孔子求教。孔子説:“如果您不貪圖財貨,就是獎賞他們,他們也不會去偷竊。”

12·19 季康子問政於孔子曰:“如殺無道,以就有道,何如?”孔子對曰:“子爲政,焉用殺?子欲善而民善矣。君子之德風,小人之德草。草上之風,必偃。”

【譯文】季康子向孔子求教怎樣治理國家,説:“假若殺掉壞人來親近好人,怎麽樣?”孔子回答説:“您治理國家哪裏一定用得着殺人?您想搞好,百姓自然會好。領導人的德行好比是風,

12. 14 Zizhang asked about government. The Master said, "To be tireless and faithful in carrying on your government."

12. 15 The Master said, "He who is widely versed in letters and keeps himself under the restraint of propriety may thus not overstep what is right."

12. 16 The Master said, "A superior man helps fulfil other's cherished hopes; he does not help fulfil other's cherished evils. The small man does the opposite of this."

12. 17 Ji Kang Zi asked Confucius about government, The Master said, "To rule is to set straight. If you give an upright lead, who will dare walk crooked?"

12. 18 Ji Kang Zi, being vexed by thieves, spoke of it to Confucius. Confucius said, "If you, sir, were not greedy, though you should reward thieves, no one would steal."

12. 19 Ji Kang Zi asked Confucius about government, saying, "What do you think of killing the bad so as to help on the good?" Confucius answered, "Sir, in carring on your government, why should you use killing at all? Were you set on good, sir, your people would do good. The superiors' virtue is the wind, the inferiors' virtue is grass. Wherever the wind

老百姓的德行好比是草。風從草上吹過，草必定向一邊倒。”

12·20 子張問："士何如斯可謂之達矣？"子曰："何哉，爾所謂達者？"子張對曰："在邦必聞，在家必聞。"子曰："是聞也，非達也。夫達也者，質直而好義，察言而觀色，慮以下人。在邦必達，在家必達。夫聞也者，色取仁而行違，居之不疑。在邦必聞，在家必聞。"

【譯文】子張問："讀書人怎樣做才能叫通達？"孔子說："你所說的通達是什么意思？"子張說："在國家的職位上一定有名望，作大夫的家臣一定有名望。"孔子說："這是名望，不是通達。怎樣才能叫通達呢？品質正直，遇事做得合情理，善於分析別人的話語，觀察別人的顏色，每每考慮到謙讓，不居於別人之上。這種人，在國家的職位上一定事事行得通，在大夫家臣的職位上也一定事事行得通。至于所謂有名望，表面上似乎愛好仁德，實際行為背道而馳，自己卻以仁人自居，而不加懷疑。這種人，在國家的職位上一定會騙取名望，在大夫家臣的職位上也一定會騙取名望。"

12·21 樊遲從遊於舞雩之下，曰："敢問崇德，修慝，辨惑。"子曰："善哉問！先事後得，非崇德與？攻其惡，無攻人之惡，非修慝與？一朝之忿，忘其身，以及其親，非惑與？"

【譯文】樊遲陪侍孔子在舞雩臺下遊覽，說："我大膽地問，怎樣去提高自己的品德，消除別人不曾表露出來的隱怨，辨別哪些是糊塗事。"孔子說："問得好！工作在先，收獲在後，這不足以提高自己的品德嗎？抨擊自己的壞處，不抨擊別人的壞處，這不就可以消除隱怨嗎？因為一時偶然的憤怒，便忘掉自己，甚至也忘掉父母，豈不是糊塗嗎？"

blows, grass bends."

12. 20 Zi Zhang asked, "When may a scholar be called eminent?" The Master said, "What do you mean by eminence?" Zizhang answered, "It is to be heard of through the state, and to be heard of through the family." The Master said, "That is fame, not eminence. The eminent man is straightforward, and loves righteousness. He examines man's words and observes their expressions. He bears in mind the necessity of deferring to others. Such a man will be eminent in the state, and eminent in the family. A famous man wears a mask of righteousness, his conduct belies it. And he rests in this character without doubts about himself. Such a man will be heard of in the state, he will be heard of in the family."

12. 21 While wandering through the Wuyu altar with the Master, Fan Chi said to him, "May I ask how to exalt virtue, to remove hidden resentment, and discover delusions?" The Master said, "A good question! Rate the task above the prize, will not the virtue be exalted? Assail one's owe evil, not the evil of others, will not hidden resentment be removed? For a morning's anger, to disregard one's life, and involve that of parents, is not this a case of delusion?"

12·22 樊遲問仁。子曰:“愛人。”問知。子曰:“知人。”

樊遲未達。子曰:“舉直錯諸枉,能使枉者直。”

樊遲退,見子夏曰:“鄉也吾見於夫子而問知,子曰‘舉直錯諸枉,能使枉者直’,何謂也?”

子夏曰:“富哉言乎!舜有天下,選於衆,舉皋陶,不仁者遠矣。湯有天下,選於衆,舉伊尹,不仁者遠矣。”

【譯文】樊遲問什麼是仁。孔子説:“愛護别人。”他又問什麼是智。孔子説:“善於鑒别人物。”

樊遲不很理解。孔子説:“提拔正直的人,官位在不正派的人之上,便能使不正派的人也正直。”

樊遲退了出來,看見子夏,説:“剛才我見到老師,問什麼是智,他老人家説,‘提拔正直的人,官位在不正派的人之上,能使不正派的人也正直。’這是什麼意思?”

子夏説:“這話的意義多麼豐富呀!舜得天下,在衆人中挑選人才,任用皋陶,不仁的人就遠離了。湯得天下,在衆人中挑選人才,任用伊尹,不仁的人就遠離了。”

12·23 子貢問友。子曰:“忠告而善道之,不可則止,毋自辱焉。”

【譯文】子貢問怎樣對待朋友。孔子説:“誠心誠意地告誡他,好心地開導他,他不聽就算了,不要自找侮辱。”

12·24 曾子曰:“君子以文會友,以友輔仁。”

【譯文】曾子説:“君子用文章學問來聚會朋友,憑藉朋友來幫助自己培養仁德。”

12. 22 Fan Chi asked about human-heartedness. The Master said, "To love all people. "He asked about wisdom. The Master said, "To know all people. "

Fan Chi did not understand. The Master said, "Promote the upright and put them above the crooked, the crooked can be made to be upright. "

Fan Chi withdrew, meeting Zixia, said to him, "Just now I had an interview with our Master and asked him about wisdom. The Master said, 'Promote the upright, put them above the crooked; the crooked can be made to be upright. ' What did he mean?"

Zixia said, "How rich is his saying! When Shun was in possession of the world, he chose Gao Yao from the many, exalted him, and men without virtue disappeared. When Tang was in possession of the world, he chose Yi Yin from the many, exalted him, and men without virtue disappeared. "

12. 23 Zigong asked about friends. The Master said, "Faithfully admonish him, and kindly guide them. If this proves vain, stop. Do not disgrace yourself. "

12. 24 Zeng Zi said, "A superior man gathers friends on literary grounds, and props his virtue by their friendship. "

子路篇第十三

13·1 子路問政。子曰："先之勞之。"請益。曰："無倦。"

【譯文】子路問怎樣治理國家。孔子說："凡事身先下屬，身體力行，然后讓他們勤勞地工作。"子路請求多講一點。孔子說："做事不要懈怠。"

13·2 仲弓爲季氏宰，問政。子曰："先有司，赦小過，舉賢才。"

曰："焉知賢才而舉之？"子曰："舉爾所知；爾所不知，人其舍諸？"

【譯文】仲弓做季氏的總管，問怎樣管理政務。孔子說："給有關工作人員帶頭，不計較人家小的過失，推薦優秀人才。"

仲弓說："怎麼知道誰是優秀人才而加以推舉呢？"孔子說："推舉你所知道的。你所不知道的，別人難道會把他埋沒嗎？"

13·3 子路曰："衛君待子而爲政，子將奚先？"

子曰："必也正名乎！"

子路曰："有是哉，子之迂也！奚其正？"

子曰："野哉，由也！君子於其所不知，蓋闕如也。名不正，則言不順；言不順，則事不成；事不成，則禮樂不興；禮樂不興，則刑罰不中；刑罰不中，則民無所措手足。故君子名之必可言也，言之必可行也。君子於其言，無所苟而已矣。"

【譯文】子路說："衛國君主等待您去治理國政，您首先幹什麼呢？"

孔子說："一定糾正名分上的用詞不當吧！"

子路說："您竟迂腐到這種程度啊！這有什么糾正的必要

BOOK XIII ZI LU

13. 1 Zilu asked about government. The Master said, "Take the lead and be laborious in their affairs. "Zilu requested further instruction, and was answered, "Never be weary in these things. "

13. 2 Zhonggong, being steward of the Ji family, asked about government. The Master said, "Let officers act first, pardon small faults, and promote men of virtue and talents. "

Zhonggong said, "How shall I know men of virtue and talents I have to promote?" The Master said, "Promote those you know. As to those you do not know, will others neglect them?"

13. 3 Zilu said, "The prince of Wei has been waiting for you to govern. What shall you do first?"

The Master replied, "The one thing needed first is the rectification of names. "

"Indeed! "said Zilu, "You are getting so pedantic, Sir! Why must rectify names?"

The Master said, "Zhong You, how crude you are! On matters that he does not know, a superior man shows a cautious reserve. If names are not right, what is said does not accord with the truth. When what is said does not accord with the truth, affairs cannot be carried on to success. When affairs

呢？”

孔子說：“仲由，真粗魯！君子對他所不知道的只存疑在心中。用詞不當，言語便不能順理成章；言語不順理成章，事情就辦不好；事情辦不好，國家的禮樂教化也就興辦不起來；禮樂教化興辦不起來，刑罰也就不會得當；刑罰不得當，老百姓就會不知如何是好。所以，君子用一個詞，一定有其理由可以說得出來，順理成章的話也一定可以行得通。君子對於措詞說話，沒有一點馬虎的地方才罷了。”

13·4 樊遲請學稼。子曰：“吾不如老農。”請學爲圃。曰：“吾不如老圃。”

樊遲出。子曰：“小人哉，樊須也！上好禮，則民莫敢不敬；上好義，則民莫敢不服；上好信，則民莫敢不用情。夫如是，則四方之民襁負其子而至矣，焉用稼？”

【譯文】樊遲請教種莊稼。孔子說：“我趕不上老農民。”他又請教種菜蔬。孔子說：“我趕不上老菜農。”

樊遲退了出來。孔子說：“樊遲真是個小人！在上的人講究禮節，百姓就沒有人敢不敬重的；在上的人講究情義，百姓就沒有人敢不服從的；在上的人講究誠信，百姓就沒有人敢不說真話的。做到這樣，四方的百姓都會背負着孩子來投奔你，哪裏用得着自己種莊稼呢？”

13·5 子曰：“誦《詩》三百，授之以政，不達；使於四方，不能專對；雖多，亦奚以爲？”

【譯文】孔子說：“讀了《詩經》三百篇，把政務交給他，完成不了；叫他出國辦外交，又不能獨立應對，這樣，即使詩讀得多，又有什么用處呢？”

cannot be carried on to success. When affairs cannot be carried on to success, rites and music do not flourish. When rites and music do not flourish, law and justice fail. And when law and justice fail, the people do not know how to move hand or foot. So a superior man consider it necessary that the names he uses may be spoken appropriately, and also that what he speaks may be carried out appropriately. The superior man, in what he says, leaves nothing to mere chance."

13. 4 Fan Chi asked to be taught farming. The Master said, "I am not so good at that as an old farmer." he asked to be taught gardening. The Master said, "I am not so good at that as an old gardener."

When Fan Chi left, the Master said, "A small man, indeed, is Fan Chi! If those above love propriety, the people will not dare to respect them; if those above love righteousness, the people will not dare to disobey; if those above love good faith, the people will not dare to hide the heart. Then, the people from all corners will come to him, bearing their children on their backs. What need will there be for farming?"

13. 5 The Master said, "Though a man may be able to recite the three hundred poems in the Book of Poetry, yet if, he does not know how to act when put to govern; if, he cannot answer for himself when sent on a mission to other states; despite the extent of his learning, of what use is it to him?"

13. 6 The Master said, "When a ruler's personal conduct

13·6 子曰:"其身正,不令而行;其身不正,雖令不從。"

【譯文】孔子說:"本人正派,不發命令,事情也行得通。本人不正派,下達命令,别人也不會信從。"

13·7 子曰:"魯、衛之政,兄弟也。"

【譯文】孔子說:"魯國、衛國的政治,像兄弟一樣相差不遠。"

13·8 子謂衛公子荆,"善居室。始有,曰:'苟合矣。'少有,曰:'苟完矣。'富有,曰:'苟美矣。'"

【譯文】孔子談到衛國的公子荆,說:"他善於居家過日子,剛有一點家業,便說:'差不多夠用了。'稍稍增加一些,便說:'差不多完備了。'相當富足了,便說:'差不多富麗堂皇了。'"

13·9 子適衛,冉有僕。子曰:"庶矣哉!"

冉有曰:"既庶矣,又何加焉?"曰:"富之。"

曰:"既富矣,又何加焉?"曰:"教之。"

【譯文】孔子到衛國去,冉有給他駕車。孔子說:"衛國人口好多呀!"

冉有說:"人口多了,又該幹什麼呢?"孔子說:"讓他們富足。"

冉有又說:"他們富足了,又該幹什麼呢?"孔子說:"教育他們。"

13·10 子曰:"苟有用我者,期月而已可也,三年有成。"

【譯文】孔子說:"假如有人要我主持國家政事,一年可以初見成效,三年會大見成效。"

13·11 子曰:"'善人爲邦百年,亦可以勝殘去殺矣。'誠哉

is correct, his government is effective without giving orders. If his personal conduct is not correct, even he may give orders, but they will not be followed."

13. 7 The Master said, "In their politics Lu and Wei are brothers."

13. 8 Speaking of grandee Jing of the Wei State, the Master said, "He knew the economy of a family well, when he began to have means, he said, 'This is much.' When he grew better off, he said, 'This is fairly complete.' And when he was rich, he said, 'We live in splender.'"

13. 9 When the Master went to Wei, Ran You drove the carriage for him. The Master said, "What a dense population!"

Ran You said, "Since the people are already numerous, What next should be done for them?" The Master said, "Enrich them."

"And when they have been enriched, what next should be done for them?" The Master said, "Teach them."

13. 10 The Master said, "If I were employed in the government, in twelve months, all would win initial success. In three years, all would achieve remarkable success."

13. 11 The Master said, "'If good men were to govern a country for a hundred years, it would be really possible to stop

是言也！”

【譯文】孔子說：“‘好人治理國家，連續一百年，也可以克服殘暴，免除虐殺了。’這句話說得真對呀！”

13·12 子曰：“如有王者，必世而後仁。”

【譯文】孔子說：“如果有以德服人的聖君出現，也要經過三十年，才能實行仁政。”

13·13 子曰：“苟正其身矣，於從政乎何有？不能正其身，如正人何？”

【譯文】孔子說：“如果自身端正了，對治理國政有什么困難呢？連本身都不能端正，怎樣能端正別人呢？”

13·14 冉子退朝。子曰：“何晏也？”對曰：“有政。”子曰：“其事也。如有政，雖不吾以，吾其與聞之。”

【譯文】冉有從公廷回來。孔子說：“為什麼回來這么晚？”冉有回答說：“有政務要辦。”孔子說：“那只是事務罷了。假若有政務要辦，雖然不用我，我也會知道。”

13·15 定公問：“一言而可以興邦，有諸？”

孔子對曰：“言不可以若是其幾也。人之言曰：‘爲君難，爲臣不易。’如知爲君之難也，不幾乎一言而興邦乎？”

曰：“一言而喪邦，有諸？”

孔子對曰：“言不可以若是其幾也。人之言曰：‘予無樂乎爲君，唯其言而莫予違也。’如其善而莫之違也，不亦善乎？如不善而莫之違也，不幾乎一言而喪邦乎？”

【譯文】魯定公問：“一句話可以使國家興盛，有這回事嗎？”

孔子回答說：“話不能說得這樣簡單。有人說：‘做國君難，做

cruelty and do away with slaughter. 'True indeed is this saying!"

13. 12 The Master said, "If a truly royal ruler were to arise, within thirty years virtue would prevail."

13. 13 The Master said, "If a ruler makes his own conduct correct, what difficulty will he have in governing? If he cannot rectify himself, what has he to do with rectifying others?"

13. 14 As the disciple Ran You came back from the court, the Master said to him, "Why are you so late?" he answered, "I had government affairs." The Master said, "It must have been general affairs. If there had been government affairs, though I am not used, I should have been heard of it."

13. 15 Duke Ding asked, "Is there any one saying that can make a state prosperous?"

Confucius answered, "It cannot be said so simply. However, there is a saying which people have, 'To be a prince is difficult, to be a minister is not easy.' And did one know how difficult it is to be a prince, might not this one saying all but make a state prosperous?"

The duke said, "Is there any one saying that can ruin a state?"

Confucius answered, "It cannot be said so simply. Howev-

臣子也不容易。'如果知道做國君的艱難,不是近乎一句話便能使國家興盛嗎?"

魯定公又問:"一句話可以喪失國家,有這回事麼?"

孔子回答說:"話不能說得這樣簡單。有人說:'我做國君沒有別的樂趣,唯一高興的是我說話沒有人違抗。'假若說的話正確而沒有人違抗,不也好嗎?假若說得不正確,也沒有人違抗,不是近於一句話就可以喪失國家嗎?"

13·16 葉公問政。子曰:"近者悅,遠者來。"

【譯文】葉公問怎樣管理政事。孔子說:"讓近處的人感到高興,讓遠方的人來投奔你。"

13·17 子夏爲莒父宰,問政。子曰:"無欲速,無見小利。欲速,則不達;見小利,則大事不成。"

【譯文】子夏做莒父的縣長,問怎樣治理。孔子說:"不要急於求成,不要顧及小利益。想要快,就反而不能達到預期的目的;顧及小利益,就辦不成大事。"

13·18 葉公語孔子曰:"吾黨有直躬者,其父攘羊,而子證之。"孔子曰:"吾黨之直者異於是:父爲子隱,子爲父隱,直在其中矣。"

【譯文】葉公告訴孔子說:"我那裏有個坦白直率的人,他父親偷了羊,這兒子便去告發。"孔子說:"我家鄉坦白直率的人和這不同,父親替兒子隱瞞,兒子替父親隱瞞,坦白直率就包含在這裏面了。"

13·19 樊遲問仁。子曰:"居處恭,執事敬,與人忠。雖之夷狄,不可棄也。"

er, there is a saying which people have, 'I have no pleasure in being a prince, only in that no one oppose what I say.' If a prince's words are right, and no one opposes them, is it not good? But if they are not right, and no one opposes them, might not this one saying all but ruin a state?"

13. 16 The Duke of She asked about government. The Master said, "To gladden those around you and attract men from afar."

13. 17 Zixia, being governor of Jufu, asked about government. The Master said, "Do not desire to have things done quickly; do not covert small advantages. Desire to have things done quickly prevents their being done thoroughly. Coverting small advantages prevents important things from being accomplished."

13. 18 The Duke of She told Confucius, "In my hometown there is a upright man. His father stole a sheep, he born witness against him." Confucius said, "In my hometown, the people's uprightness is unlike that. The father screens his son, the son screens his father. Uprightness is in this."

13. 19 Fan Chi asked about perfect virtue. The Master said, "To be respectful at home, painstaking at work, faithful to all. Even among rude uncultivated tribes, none of this may

【譯文】樊遲問什麼是仁。孔子說:"平日在家容貌態度端莊,辦事情嚴肅認真,為別人做事誠心實意。這幾種品德,即使到夷狄地區也是不可拋棄的。"

13·20 子貢問曰:"何如斯可謂之士矣?"子曰:"行己有恥,使於四方,不辱君命,可謂士矣。"

曰:"敢問其次。"曰:"宗族稱孝焉,鄉黨稱弟焉。"

曰:"敢問其次。"曰:"言必信,行必果,硜硜然小人哉!抑亦可以爲次矣。"

曰:"今之從政者何如?"子曰:"噫!斗筲之人,何足算也?"

【譯文】子貢問:"怎樣才能叫'士'呢?"孔子說:"自己行事知道羞恥,出使外國能很好完成國君交給的使命,可以叫做'士'了。"

子貢問:"請問次一等的呢?"孔子說:"本宗族的人稱贊他孝順父母,本鄉本地的人稱贊他尊敬長者。"

子貢又問:"再次一等的呢?"孔子說:"說話一定講信用,做事一定果斷,這是不問是非曲直只求貫徹自己言行的小人呀,但也可以說是再次一等的'士'了。"

子貢又問:"現在這些在位的人怎樣?"孔子說:"唉!胸襟狹小的人,算得了什麼呀?"

13·21 子曰:"不得中行而與之,必也狂狷乎!狂者進取,狷者有所不爲也。"

【譯文】孔子說:"不能與言行中庸的人交往,那只有和激進的人或潔身自好的人相交吧!激進的人勇於進取,潔身自好的人不去幹壞事。"

13·22 子曰:"南人有言曰:'人而無恒,不可以作巫醫。'

be dropped."

13.20 Zigong asked, "What qualities must a man possess to be called a superior man?" The Master said, "He who maintains a sense of shame in his personal conduct; and when sent to any state does not disgrace his prince's commission, may be called a superior man."

Zigong said, "May I ask who would rank next?" The Master said, "The man whom his clansmen praised for his filial piety, his villagers praised for his respect to the elders."

Again Zigong asked, "May I ask who would rank next?" The Master said, "He who is determined to do what he says, and to carry out what he does, never minds they are right or not, a obstinate small man, yet perhaps would come next."

Zigong asked, "How are those who engage in government today?" The Master said, "Pooh! These narrow-minded small men, not worth being taken into account."

13.21 The Master said, "Since I cannot get men pursuing the golden mean to communicate with, I must find the ardent and the cautiously-decided. The ardent will press forward, the cautiously-decided will keep themselves from what is wrong."

13.22 The Master said, "The people of the south have a saying--- 'A man without constancy even cannot make a wiz-

善夫!”

“不恒其德,或承之羞。”子曰:“不占而已矣。”

【譯文】孔子說:“南方人有句話:‘人如果没有恒心,連巫醫都做不了。’這話真好呀!”

《易經》説:“不長期堅守自己的道德,總有人招致羞辱。”孔子又説:“這是叫無恒心的人不必去占卦。”

13·23 子曰:“君子和而不同,小人同而不和。”

【譯文】孔子説:“君子講究互相協調,而不盲目隨從;小人則盲目隨從,而不講究協調。”

13·24 子貢問曰:“鄉人皆好之,何如?”子曰:“未可也。”

“鄉人皆惡之,何如?”子曰:“未可也;不如鄉人之善者好之,其不善者惡之。”

【譯文】子貢問道:“一鄉的人都喜歡他,這人怎麼樣?”孔子說:“不一定好。”

子貢又問:“一鄉的人都厭惡他,這人怎麼樣?”孔子說:“不一定壞。最好是一鄉的好人喜歡他,壞人厭惡他。”

13·25 子曰:“君子易事而難説也。説之不以道,不説也;及其使人也,器之。小人難事而易説也。説之雖不以道,説也;及其使人也,求備焉。”

【譯文】孔子說:“在君子手下工作容易,討他的歡喜卻難。不用正當的方式去討他喜歡,他是不會喜歡的;等到他使喚人的時候,衡量各人的才德去分配任務。在小人手下工作難,討他喜歡卻容易。用不正當的方式討他喜歡,他也會喜歡,等到他使喚人的時候,便百般挑剔,求全責備。”

ard-doctor. 'Well said!"

The Books of Change says "Inconstant in his virtue, he will incur disgrace." The Master said, "What this sentence means is that those without constancy need not go to divine."

13.23 The Master said, "The superior man is conciliatory but not blind-accommodating; the small man is blind-accommodating but not conciliatory."

13.24 Zigong asked, "What do you say of a man who is loved by all his fellow-villagers?" The Master said, "That is not enough."

"And what do you say of a man who is hated by all his fellow-villagers?" The Master said, "That is not enough. Best of all would be that the good in the village love him and the bad hate him."

13.25 The Master said, "A superior man is easy to serve and difficult to please. If you try to please him in any manner which is not accordant with the Way, he will not be pleased. But in his employment of men, he uses them according to their capacity. The small man is difficult to serve and easy to please. If you try to please him, even though in a manner which is not accordant with the Way, he will be pleased. But in his employment of men, he expects them to do any work that comes along."

13.26 The Master said, "The superior man has dignified

13·26　子曰："君子泰而不驕，小人驕而不泰。"

【譯文】孔子説："君子安詳舒展，而不傲慢；小人傲慢，而不安詳舒展。"

13·27　子曰："剛、毅、木、訥近仁。"

【譯文】孔子説："剛強、果斷、質樸、言語謹慎，具有這四種品德的人接近於仁。"

13·28　子路問曰："何如斯可謂之士矣？"子曰："切切偲偲，怡怡如也，可謂士矣。朋友切切偲偲，兄弟怡怡。"

【譯文】子路問道："怎樣才可以稱做'士'？"孔子説："互相懇切地批評勉勵，和睦共處，可以稱做'士'了。朋友之間，應互相懇切地批評勉勵，兄弟之間應和睦共處。"

13·29　子曰："善人教民七年，亦可以即戎矣。"

【譯文】孔子説："善人教導人民七年，也可以叫他們去作戰了。"

13·30　子曰："以不教民戰，是謂棄之。"

【譯文】孔子説："用没有受過軍事訓練的人民去作戰，這叫做拋棄他們。"

憲問篇第十四

14·1　憲問恥。子曰："邦有道，穀；邦無道，穀，恥也。"

"克、伐、怨、欲不行焉，可以爲仁矣？"子曰："可以爲難矣，仁則吾不知也。"

【譯文】原憲問什麼是恥辱。孔子説："國家政治清平，做官拿

ease, but without pride; the small man has pride, but without dignified ease."

13.27 The Master said, "Fortitude, resolution, simplicity and caution in speech are near to the perfect virtue."

13.28 Zilu asked, "What qualities must a man possess to be called a superior man?" The Master said, "A man who is earnest and encouraging, kind and bland may be called a superior man. Among his friends, earnest and encouraging; among his brothers, kind and bland."

13.29 The Master said, "Could a good man instruct the people for seven years, they would be fit for arms also."

13.30 The Master said, "To lead untrained men into war, is to throw them away."

BOOK XIV XIAN WENG

14.1 Yuan Xuan① asked what was shameful. The Master said, "When the Way prevails in the state, to take office and accept salary; and when the Way does not prevail in the state, still to take office and accept salary, this is shameful."

"To eschew the love of mastery, boasting, resentment and

---

① i.e. Yuan Si.

俸穀;國家腐敗黑暗,做官也拿俸穀,這就是恥辱。”

原憲又說:“好勝、自誇、怨恨和貪心都沒有表現過,可以說是仁了吧?”孔子說:“可以說是難能可貴了,是否仁,我不知道。”

14·2 子曰:“士而懷居,不足以爲士矣。”

【譯文】孔子說:“士如果留戀安逸生活,便不足以成為士了。”

14·3 子曰:“邦有道,危言危行;邦無道,危行言孫。”

【譯文】孔子說:“國家政治清平,說話正直,行為正直;國家腐敗黑暗,行為正直,說話謙順。”

14·4 子曰:“有德者必有言,有言者不必有德。仁者必有勇,勇者不必有仁。”

【譯文】孔子說:“有道德的人一定有名言;有名言的人卻不一定有道德。仁德的人一定勇敢,勇敢的人卻不一定有仁德。”

14·5 南宮适問於孔子曰:“羿善射,奡盪舟,俱不得其死然。禹稷躬稼而有天下。”夫子不答。

南宮适出,子曰:“君子哉若人!尚德哉若人!”

【譯文】南宮适問孔子說:“羿擅長射箭,奡擅長水戰,都沒有得到好死。禹和稷親自下地種田,得到了天下。”孔子沒有回答。

南宮适出來後,孔子說:“這個人是個君子啊!這個人多么崇尚道德啊!”

14·6 子曰:“君子而不仁者有矣夫,未有小人而仁者也。”

【譯文】孔子說:“君子當中有不仁德的人吧,小人當中卻不會有仁德的人。”

greed, can that be called perfect virtue?" The Master said, "That may be called what is difficult to do, But whether it should be called perfect virtue I do not know."

14. 2 The Master said, "The superior man who cherishes only the love of comfort is not worthy the name."

14. 3 The Master said, "When the Way prevails in the state, be upright in speech and upright in action; when the Way does not prevail, be upright in action but modest in speech."

14. 4 The Master said, "A man of virtue will be sure to possess eloquence, but those who possess eloquence may not always be men of virtue. A man of human-heartedness will be sure to possess courage, but those who possess courage may not always be men of human-heartedness."

14. 5 Nangong Kuo said to Confucius, "Yi was good at archery, Ao could move a boat overland, but neither of them died a natural death. Yu and Ji personally toiled at their crops and won the world." The Master made no reply.

But when Nangong Kuo went out, the Master said, "What a superior man he is! How he prizes virtue!"

14. 6 The Master said, "Superior men, and yet without human-heartedness, there may be. But there never has been a small man with human-heartedness."

14·7　子曰："愛之，能勿勞乎？忠焉，能勿誨乎？"

【譯文】孔子說："愛他，能夠不讓他勞累嗎？對他效忠竭力，能夠不教誨他嗎？"

14·8　子曰："爲命，裨諶草創之，世叔討論之，行人子羽修飾之，東里子產潤色之。"

【譯文】孔子說："鄭國的法令文件，由裨諶擬稿，世叔提意見，外交官子羽修改潤飾，東里的子產作文辭上的加工。"

14·9　或問子產。子曰："惠人也。"

問子西。曰："彼哉！彼哉！"

問管仲。曰："人也。奪伯氏駢邑三百，飯疏食，沒齒無怨言。"

【譯文】有人問子產怎麼樣。孔子說："是位仁慈恩惠的人。"

又問子西怎麼樣。孔子說："他呀，他呀！"

又問到管仲怎麼樣。孔子說："是個人才。他剝奪了伯氏封地三百戶的駢邑，自己只吃粗糧，到死沒有一句怨恨的話。"

14·10　子曰："貧而無怨難，富而無驕易。"

【譯文】孔子說："貧困卻沒有怨恨是很難的，富貴卻不驕傲是容易的。"

14·11　子曰："孟公綽爲趙、魏老則優，不可以爲滕、薛大夫。"

【譯文】孔子說："孟公綽做晉國大臣趙家、魏家的總管，能力有餘，卻不能做滕、薛這樣小國的大夫。"

14·12　子路問成人。子曰："若臧武仲之知，公綽之不欲，

14. 7 The Master said, "Can there be love which does not lead to the toil of its object? Can there be loyalty which does not lead to the instruction of its object?"

14. 8 The Master said, "In preparing the decrees, Bi Chen first made the rough draft; Shishu checked and revised it; Ziyu, the manager of foreign affairs, amended it; and Zichan of Dong Li polished it and gave it the proper elegance."

14. 9 Someone asked about Zichan. The Master said, "He was a kind-hearted man."

He asked about Zixi. The Master said, "That man! That man!"

Asked about Guang Zhong, the Master said, "He was the man of ability. He took the town of Pian with its three hundred households from its owner Bo; yet Bo, though he had only coarse rice to eat till his death, could find no word of resentment to say."

14. 10 The Master said, "To be poor without resentment is difficult; to be rich without being proud is easier."

14. 11 The Master said, "Meng Gongchuo is more than fit to be steward to the Zhao and Wei families, but he is not fit to be minister of either Teng or Xue State."

14. 12 Zilu asked what was meant by 'a perfect man'.

卞莊子之勇,冉求之藝,文之以禮樂,亦可以爲成人矣。”曰:“今之成人者何必然?見利思義,見危授命,久要不忘平生之言,亦可以爲成人矣。”

【譯文】子路問怎麼樣才是一個完美無缺的人。孔子說:“聰明智慧像臧武仲,清心寡慾像孟公綽,勇敢像卞莊子,多才多藝像冉求,再用禮樂來增加他的文采,可以說是完美無缺的人了。”又說:“現在完美無缺的人哪裏一定要這樣,看見利益能想到道義,碰到危險願獻出生命,長期窮困而不忘記平日的諾言,這樣也可以說是完美無缺的人了。”

14·13 子問公叔文子於公明賈曰:“信乎,夫子不言,不笑,不取乎?”

公明賈對曰:“以告者過也。夫子時然後言,人不厭其言;樂然後笑,人不厭其笑;義然後取,人不厭其取。”

子曰:“其然?豈其然乎?”

【譯文】孔子向公明賈問到公叔文子,說:“他老人家不說話,不笑,不貪取,是真的嗎?”

公明賈回答說:“這是告訴您的人說錯了。他老人家該說時才說,別人不厭惡他的話;高興了才笑,別人不討厭他的笑;合乎情理應該取的才取,別人不厭惡他的取。”

孔子說:“是這樣嗎?難道真的是這樣嗎?”

14·14 子曰:“臧武仲以防求爲後於魯,雖曰不要君,吾不信也。”

【譯文】孔子說:“臧武仲憑藉他的封地防城,向魯君要求立他的後人為卿大夫,雖說不是要挾國君,我卻不相信。”

14·15 子曰:“晉文公譎而不正,齊桓公正而不譎。”

The Master said, "A man wise as Zang Wuzhong, uncovetous as Meng Gongchuo, bold as Bian Zhuang Zi, gifted as Ran Qiu, and graced with the rules of propriety and music, might be called a perfect man." He then added, "But today who askes all these of a perfect man? The man, who in sight of gain remembers righteousness, in face of danger will risk his life, in the long-standing poverty will cleave to his promise, may be called a perfect man."

14. 13 The Master asked Gongming Jia about Gongshu Wen Zi, saying, "Is it true that he does not speak, nor laugh, nor take?"

Gongming Jia replied, "The man who told you this was exaggerating. The Master speaks when it is the time to speak, so none is weary of his speaking; he laughs when he is joyful, so none is weary of his laughter; he takes what is right to take, so none is weary of his taking."

The Master said, "Was that so? Can that really have been so?"

14. 14 The Master said, "Zang Wuzhong, holding the fief of Fang, asked the prince of Lu to appoint his descendants as senior officials in Lu. Though it was said that he was not forcing his prince, I cannot believe it."

14. 15 The Master said, "Duke Wen of Jin was crafty

【譯文】孔子說："晉文公詭詐而不正派；齊桓公正派而不詭詐。"

14·16 子路曰："桓公殺公子糾，召忽死之，管仲不死。"曰："未仁乎？"子曰："桓公九合諸侯，不以兵車，管仲之力也。如其仁，如其仁。"

【譯文】子路說："齊桓公殺了公子糾，召忽也自殺了，管仲卻不死。"又說："管仲可說是沒有仁德吧？"孔子說："齊桓公多次聚集各國君主結盟，不用武力，都是管仲出的力。這就是他的仁德！這就是他的仁德！"

14·17 子貢曰："管仲非仁者與？桓公殺公子糾，不能死，又相之。"子曰："管仲相桓公，霸諸侯，一匡天下，民到于今受其賜。微管仲，吾其被髮左衽矣。豈若匹夫匹婦之爲諒也，自經於溝瀆而莫之知也？"

【譯文】子貢說："管仲不是一個有仁德的人吧？桓公殺了公子糾，管仲不自殺，又去輔佐齊桓公。"孔子說："管子輔佐齊桓公，稱霸諸侯，匡正天下，百姓到今天還蒙受他的好處。假使沒有管仲，我們都會披散頭髮，衣襟向左邊開，(淪為落後民族了。)他難道也要像普通人那樣，守着小節小信在山溝中上吊自殺，而沒有人知道嗎？"

14·18 公叔文子之臣大夫僎與文子同升諸公。子聞之，曰："可以爲'文'矣。"

【譯文】公叔文子的家臣大夫僎，由於文子向朝廷推薦他，和文子一同做了大臣。孔子聽到這件事，說："文子可以得到'文'的謚號了。"

and not upright. Duke Huan of Qi was upright and not crafty."

14.16 Zilu said, "When Duke Huan of Qi slew his brother grandee Jiu, Zhao Hu died with him, but Guan Zhong did not. Was he not want in virtue?" The Master said, "The Duke Huan was able to convene the princes of all the states without resorting to the use of weapons and chariots of war; it was all due to Guan Zhong. Such is his virtue! Such is his virtue!"

14.17 Zigong said, "Guan Zhong, I think, was not a man of virtue. When Duke Huan slew his brother Prince Jiu, Guan Zhong did not die with him, moreover he became prime minister to Huan." The Master said, "By Guan Zhong's help, Duke Huan became leader of all the feudal princes, and united and rectified the whole world. Down to the present day the people have benefited from what he then did. But for Guan Zhong, we should now wear our hair dishevelled and fold our clothes to the left. Will you except from him the small fidelity of common men and common women, who would commit suicide in a stream or ditch, no one knowing about them?"

14.18 Gongshu Wen Zi became a minister of Wei together with his retainer Xun. When the Master heard of this, he said, "He deserves to be called Wen (cultured)."

14·19　子言衛靈公之無道也,康子曰:“夫如是,奚而不喪?”孔子曰:“仲叔圉治賓客,祝鮀治宗廟,王孫賈治軍旅。夫如是,奚其喪?”

【譯文】孔子談到衛靈公的昏庸無道,季康子說:“他既然這樣,為什麼没有滅亡呢?”孔子說:“他有仲叔圉接待賓客,祝鮀管理祭祀,王孫賈統率軍隊。像這樣,怎麼會滅亡?”

14·20　子曰:“其言之不怍,則爲之也難。”

【譯文】孔子說:“一個人大言不慚,他做起來就不容易。”

14·21　陳成子弑簡公。孔子沐浴而朝,告於哀公曰:“陳恒弑其君,請討之。”公曰:“告夫三子!”

孔子曰:“以吾從大夫之後,不敢不告也。君曰‘告夫三子’者!”

之三子告,不可。孔子曰:“以吾從大夫之後,不敢不告也。”

【譯文】陳成子殺了齊簡公。孔子沐浴齋戒後去上朝,報告魯哀公說:“陳恒殺了他的君主,請求您討伐他。”魯哀公說:“你告訴季孫、仲孫、孟孫三位大臣吧!”

孔子退朝後說:“我曾忝列大夫之官,不敢不報告,君主卻說:‘告訴那三位去吧!’”

孔子又到三位大夫那裏去報告,三位大夫不同意。孔子說:“我曾忝列大夫之官,不敢不來報告。”

14·22　子路問事君。子曰:“勿欺也,而犯之。”

【譯文】子路問怎樣服侍國君。孔子說:“不要欺騙,但可以當面直言觸犯他。”

14·23　子曰:“君子上達,小人下達。”

14.19 When the Master said that Duke Ling of Wei did not follow the right way, Ji Kang Zi asked, "Since he is like that, why has he not lost his throne?" Confucius answered, "He has Zhongshu Yu to deal with foreign envoys and guests, Zhu Tuo in charge of the ancestral temple, and Wangsun Jia to command the army, how should he lose his throne?"

14.20 The Master said, "He who speaks without modesty will find it difficult to put his words into practice."

14.21 When Chen Cheng Zi murdered Duke Jian of Qi, Confucius bathed, went to court, and told Duke Ai, saying, "Chen Heng has slain his prince. Please dispatch troops to punish him." The duke said, "Inform the three chiefs."

Confucius said, "Following in the wake of the great officers, I dared not to leave such a matter untold. But the prince says, 'Inform the three chiefs.'"

He then informed the three chiefs. They refused to act. Confucius said, "Following in the wake of the great officers, I dared not to leave such a matter untold."

14.22 Zilu asked how to serve a prince. The Master said, "Never cheat him; withstand him to his face."

14.23 The Master said, "A superior man has a complete

【譯文】孔子說："君子向上，通達仁義；小人向下，追求財利。"

14·24 子曰："古之學者爲己，今之學者爲人。"

【譯文】孔子說："古代人學習是為了提高自己，現在的人學習是為了給別人看。"

14·25 蘧伯玉使人於孔子。孔子與之坐而問焉，曰："夫子何爲？"對曰："夫子欲寡其過而未能也。"

使者出。子曰："使乎！使乎！"

【譯文】蘧伯玉派一位使者去拜訪孔子。孔子給他一個席位，問道："他老人家幹些什麼？"使者回答說："他老人家想要減少失誤，卻還沒能做到。"

使者出來後。孔子說："好一位使者！好一位使者！"

14·26 子曰："不在其位，不謀其政。"

曾子曰："君子思不出其位。"

【譯文】孔子說："不在那個職位，不考慮那方面的政事。"

曾子說："君子思考的問題不超越他的職務範圍。"

14·27 子曰："君子恥其言而過其行。"

【譯文】孔子說："君子認為所說的超過了所做的是可恥的。"

14·28 子曰："君子道者三，我無能焉：仁者不憂，知者不惑，勇者不懼。"子貢曰："夫子自道也。"

【譯文】孔子說："君子為人要做的有三件，我沒有做到：仁德的人不憂愁，智慧的人不迷惑，勇敢的人不畏懼。"子貢說："這正是老師的自我表述。"

understanding of righteousness; the small man has a complete understanding of profit."

14.24 The Master said, "In ancient times men learned for the sake of self-improvement; nowadays men learn for show."

14.25 Qu Boyu sent a messenger to Confucius. Confucius sat with him and asked, "What is the master doing?" The messenger replied, "He is trying to make his faults few, but he has not yet succeed."

When the messenger had left, the Master said, "What a messenger! What a messenger!"

14.26 The Master said, "He who is not in any particular office does not discuss its policies."

Zeng Zi said, "The superior man does not think of more than his own duties."

14.27 The Master said, "The superior man is ashamed to speak more and do less."

14.28 The Master said, "The ways of the superior man are three, but I have met with success in none of them. The virtuous is free from anxieties; the wise is free from doubts; the bold is free from fear." Zigong said, "That is what our master say about himself."

14·29 子貢方人。子曰:“賜也賢乎哉? 夫我則不暇。”

【譯文】子貢評論別人。孔子說:“端木賜,你就夠好了嗎? 我就沒有這閒工夫。”

14·30 子曰:“不患人之不己知,患其不能也。”

【譯文】孔子說:“不擔心別人不知道自己,只擔心自己沒有能力。”

14·31 子曰:“不逆詐,不億不信,抑亦先覺者,是賢乎!”

【譯文】孔子說:“不預先懷疑別人欺詐,也不無根據地猜測別人不老實,卻能及早察覺出來,這是位賢者吧!”

14·32 微生畝謂孔子曰:“丘何爲是栖栖者與? 無乃爲佞乎?”孔子曰:“非敢爲佞也,疾固也。”

【譯文】微生畝對孔子說:“你為什麼這樣忙忙碌碌呢? 不是成了能言善辯的人嗎?”孔子說:“我不敢成為能言善辯的人,而是痛恨那種頑固不化的人。”

14·33 子曰:“驥不稱其力,稱其德也。”

【譯文】孔子說:“稱千里馬叫驥,不是贊美它的力氣,而是贊美它的品德。”

14·34 或曰:“以德報怨,何如?”子曰:“何以報德?以直報怨,以德報德。”

【譯文】有人說:“用恩德來報答怨恨,怎麼樣?”孔子說:“那你用什麼來報答恩德呢?應該用正直來報答怨恨,用恩德來報答恩德。”

14. 29 Zigong was criticizing other people. The Master said, "Have you been perfect yourself? I myself have no time for this."

14. 30 The Master said, "I'm not concerned at men's not knowing me. I'm concerned at my own want of ability."

14. 31 The Master said, "He who does not doubt about others' deceit, nor harbors a groundless suspicion against their dishonesty, and yet can apprehend these things readily; ——is he not a man of worth?"

14. 32 Weisheng Mu said to Confucius, "Why are you so busy? Are you not wagging a glib tongue?" Confucius answered, "I dare not wag a glib tongue, but I hate stubbornness."

14. 33 The Master said, "A steed is not praised for its strength, but praised for its good qualities."

14. 34 Someone said, "To requite resentment with kindness, what do you think of that?" The Master said, "With what then will you requite kindness? Requite resentment with justice; requite kindness with kindness."

14·35 子曰:"莫我知也夫!"子貢曰:"何爲其莫知子也?"子曰:"不怨天,不尤人,下學而上達。知我者其天乎!"

【譯文】孔子說:"沒有人知道我呀!"子貢說:"為什麼沒有人知道您呢?"孔子說:"不怨恨上天,不責備別人,學習平常知識,透徹瞭解高深的道理。知道我的只是上天吧!"

14·36 公伯寮愬子路於季孫。子服景伯以告,曰:"夫子固有惑志於公伯寮,吾力猶能肆諸市朝。"

子曰:"道之將行也與,命也;道之將廢也與,命也。公伯寮其如命何!"

【譯文】公伯寮在季孫氏面前毀謗子路。子服景伯告訴孔子,說:"他老人家已經被公伯寮迷惑了,我還有力量殺了他陳尸街頭示衆。"

孔子說:"我的主張將要實行,是命運決定;我的主張將被廢除,也決定于命運。公伯寮又能把命運怎么樣呢!"

14·37 子曰:"賢者辟世,其次辟地,其次辟色,其次辟言。"

子曰:"作者七人矣。"

【譯文】孔子說:"賢能的人逃避惡濁社會而隱居,次一等的人躲開最壞的地方擇地而處,再次一等的人避開某些人難看的臉色,再次一等的人避開惡言惡語。"

孔子說:"這樣做的已經有七人了。"

14·38 子路宿於石門。晨門曰:"奚自?"子路曰:"自孔氏。"曰:"是知其不可而爲之者與?"

【譯文】子路在石門住了一夜,(第二天清早進城,)早上管城

14. 35 The Master said, "Alas! no one knows me!" Zigong asked, "Why do you say that no one knows you?" The Master replied, "I do not accuse Heaven, nor do I lay the blame on men. My studies lie low, and my penetration rises high. I am known but to Heaven!"

14. 36 Gongbo Liao spoke ill of Zilu to Jisun. Zifu Jingbo told this to Confucius, saying, "The old man's mind is surely being led astray by Gongbo Liao, but I still have enough strength to expose his corpse in the market."

The Master said, "If my principles are to prevail in the world, it is the will of Heaven. If they are to fall to the ground, it is also the will of Heaven. Can Gongbo Liao fight against the will of Heaven?"

14. 37 The Master said, "Men of worth shun the world; the next best shun the land; then come men go at a look, then men go at a word."

The Master said, "Seven men did so."

14. 38 Zilu spent a night at Shimen. The gate-keeper asked him, "Where do you come from?" Zi Lu said, "From Master Kong's." "The man knows that he cannot succeed, yet

門的人問："從哪裏來？"子路說："從孔家來。"那人說："是那個明知做不到卻偏要做的人嗎？"

14·39 子擊磬於衛，有荷蕢而過孔氏之門者，曰："有心哉，擊磬乎！"既而曰："鄙哉，硜硜乎！莫己知也，斯己而已矣。深則厲，淺則揭。"

子曰："果哉！末之難矣。"

【譯文】孔子在衛國有一天敲着磬，有個挑草筐的人在門前走過，說："敲磬的是位有心人呀！"過一會兒又說："磬聲硜硜的，真鄙俗呀！（它好像在說沒有人知道我啊！）沒有人知道自己，這就算了。水深就把衣裳脫下來，水淺就撩起裙子。"

孔子說："好堅決，沒有辦法說服他了。"

14·40 子張曰："《書》云：'高宗諒陰，三年不言。'何謂也？"子曰："何必高宗，古之人皆然。君薨，百官總己以聽於冢宰三年。"

【譯文】子張說："《尚書》說：'殷高宗守孝，住在凶廬，三年不講話。'這是什麼意思？"孔子說："哪裏一定是高宗，古代人都這樣。國君死了，繼承君位的人三年不談政事，各部門官員自理政務而聽命於宰相。"

14·41 子曰："上好禮，則民易使也。"

【譯文】孔子說："在上位的人講究禮法，依禮而行，百姓就容易使喚。"

14·42 子路問君子。子曰："修己以敬。"

曰："如斯而已乎？"曰："修己以安人。"

曰："如斯而已乎？"曰："修己以安百姓。修己以安百姓，堯、

keeps on trying to do it?"said the gate-keeper.

14. 39 One day when the Master was playing Qing[1] in Wei, a man, carrying a straw basket, passed the door and said, "His heart is full, who so plays Qing!" A moment later, he added, "For shame! What a tinkling note! If no one knows you, you can just do things for yourself. When the water is deep, cross it with clothes on; when it is shallow, cross it with the clothes held up." The Master said, "How determined is he in his purpose! It is impossible to persuade him."

14. 40 Zizhang said, "The Book of History says, 'Gaozong[2], when mourning his father, did not speak for three years.' What does this mean?" The Master said, "Not Gaozong in particular. The ancients all did so. Whenever a prince died, the ministers all continued in their offices, taking their orders from the Prime Minister for three years."

14. 41 The Master said, "When rulers love the rules of propriety, the people are easy to lead."

14. 42 Zilu asked what constituted a superior man. The Master said, "A man who cultivates in himself the capacity to be diligent in his tasks."

---

① A kind of musical instrument made of stone.

② The King of the Shang dynasty.

舜其猶病諸?”

【譯文】子路問怎樣才是君子。孔子説:“修養自己,恭敬謹慎。”

子路説:“這樣就夠了嗎?”孔子説:“修養自己,使親友安樂。”

子路説:“這樣就夠了嗎?”孔子説:“修養自己,使百姓安樂。修養自己,使百姓安樂,可能堯、舜還做不到呢!”

14·43 原壤夷俟。子曰:“幼而不孫弟,長而無述焉,老而不死,是爲賊。”以杖叩其脛。

【譯文】原壤撇着兩腿坐着等孔子。孔子説:“你小時候不孝不悌,長大了毫無貢獻,老了還不死,真是個害人精。”然後用拐杖敲他小腿。

14·44 闕黨童子將命。或問之曰:“益者與?”子曰:“吾見其居於位也,見其與先生并行也。非求益者也,欲速成者也。”

【譯文】闕黨地方的一個童子來向孔子傳話。有人問孔子説:“他是求上進的人嗎?”孔子説:“我看見他坐在成年人的席位上,又看見他同長輩并肩而行。這人不是肯求上進的人,而是急於求成的人。”

衛靈公篇第十五

15·1 衛靈公問陳於孔子。孔子對曰:“俎豆之事,則嘗聞之矣;軍旅之事,未之學也。”明日遂行。

【譯文】衛靈公向孔子詢問作戰的陣勢。孔子回答説:“禮儀的事情,曾經聽説過;軍隊作戰的事情,我没有學習過。”於是第二天離開衛國。

"And is this all?"said Zilu. "He cultivates himself to give ease to others."

"And is that all?""He cultivates himself to give ease to all the people,"said the Master,"To cultivate himself to give ease to all the people,---even Yao and Shun still found it difficult."

14. 43 Yuan Rang[1] sat waiting for the Master in a sprawling position. The Master said,"You did not know the rules of propriety when young,and achieved nothing as adult. You merely live on,getting older and older. A pest indeed!" With this he hit him on the leg with his staff.

14. 44 When a boy from the village of Que was made message-bearer, someone asked, "Is he improving himself?" The Master said,"I see him sitting in the seat of a grown-up man,see him walking shoulder to shoulder with his elders. He is not one who wishes to improve himself. He was only over-anxious for quick results."

BOOK XV WEI LING GONG

15. 1 Duke Ling of Wei asked Confucius about tactics. Confucius replied, "Of sacrificial rites I have learned, but I have never studied military matters."Next day he left.

---

① A friend of Confucius.

15·2　在陳絶糧，從者病，莫能興。子路愠見曰：“君子亦有窮乎？”子曰：“君子固窮，小人窮斯濫矣。”

【譯文】孔子在陳國斷絕了糧食，跟隨的人餓得病倒了，爬不起來。子路不高興地來見孔子，說：“君子也有窮困的時候嗎？”孔子說：“君子雖窮，仍然堅持着；小人一窮，便什麽都幹得出來了。”

15·3　子曰：“賜也，女以予爲多學而識之者與？”對曰：“然，非與？”曰：“非也，予一以貫之。”

【譯文】孔子說：“端木賜！你以為我是廣泛地學習而又記得住的人嗎？”子貢回答說：“是的，難道不是這樣嗎？”孔子說：“不是的，我的學說是用一條忠恕之道貫穿着的。”

15·4　子曰：“由！知德者鮮矣。”

【譯文】孔子說：“仲由，懂得道德的人很少啊。”

15·5　子曰：“無爲而治者其舜也與？夫何爲哉？恭己正南面而已矣。”

【譯文】孔子說：“自己不幹什麽而能使天下太平的，大概只有舜吧？他幹了什麽呢？莊嚴端正地坐在朝廷上罷了。”

15·6　子張問行。子曰：“言忠信，行篤敬，雖蠻貊之邦，行矣。言不忠信，行不篤敬，雖州里，行乎哉？立則見其參於前也，在輿則見其倚於衡也，夫然後行。”子張書諸紳。

【譯文】子張問怎樣才行得通。孔子說：“說話忠誠老實，行為忠厚嚴肅，即使在蠻貊國家，也行得通。說話不忠誠講信用，行為不忠厚嚴肅，就是在本鄉本土，能行得通嗎？站立的時候，就彷彿

15. 2 In Chen provisions ran out. His followers grew too ill to rise. Zilu, with evident vexation, said, "Has even a superior man to be in such want?" The Master said, "A superior man withstands hardship, but the small man, when he is in want, gives way to unbridled license."

15. 3 The Master said, "Ci, do you think that I am a man who learns much and keeps all of them in memory?" "Yes," he answered, "Is it not so?" The Master said, "No, I string all into one principle."

15. 4 The Master said, "You, those who know virtue are few."

15. 5 The Master said, "To rule doing nothing, that was Shun's way. What did he do? He merely placed himself gravely and reverently in his imperial seat; that was all."

15. 6 Zizhang asked how to get on well. The Master said, "Be sincere and true to your every word, and serious and careful in your acts, then you will get on well, even among the rude tribes. If your words are not sincere and truthful, and your acts not serious and careful, will you get on well even in your neighborhood? Standing, see these words ranged before

看見'忠誠老實忠厚嚴肅'幾個字在眼前;在車箱裏,也彷彿看見這幾個字刻在車前面的横木上;這樣才到處行得通。"子張把這些話寫在衣帶上。

15·7　子曰:"直哉史魚!邦有道,如矢;邦無道,如矢。君子哉蘧伯玉!邦有道,則仕;邦無道,則可卷而懷之。"

【譯文】孔子說:"史魚真正直啊!國家政治清明,他像箭一樣直,國家政治黑暗,也像箭一樣直。蘧伯玉真是位君子啊!國家政治清明,就出來做官,國家政治腐敗黑暗,就把本領收藏起來。"

15·8　子曰:"可與言而不與之言,失人;不可與言而與之言,失言。知者不失人,亦不失言。"

【譯文】孔子說:"可以和他談話卻不談話,這是錯過了人;不可以和他談話卻去談話,這是浪費言語。聰明人既不錯過人,又不浪費言語。"

15·9　子曰:"志士仁人,無求生以害仁,有殺身以成仁。"

【譯文】孔子說:"志士仁人,不貪生怕死去損害仁,只有犧牲自己來成全仁。"

15·10　子貢問爲仁。子曰:"工欲善其事,必先利其器。居是邦也,事其大夫之賢者,友其士之仁者。"

【譯文】子貢問怎樣實行仁德。孔子說:"各種工匠想要搞好工作,一定先修好他的工具。住在這個國家,就要事奉那裏大夫中的賢者,結交士人中有仁德的人。"

15·11　顏淵問爲邦。子曰:"行夏之時,乘殷之輅,服周之

you; driving a carriage, see them written upon the yoke. Then you will get on well." Zizhang wrote them upon his girdle.

15.7 The Master said, "Straight and upright indeed was Shiyu! When the Way prevailed, he was straight like an arrow; when the Way did not prevail, he was straight like an arrow. A superior man indeed was Qu Boyu! When the Way prevailed he took office; when the Way did not prevail, he wrapped his talents up and hid them."

15.8 The Master said, "Not to speak to one who can be spoken with, is to waste a man. To speak to one who can not be spoken with, is to waste words. The wise never waste a man, nor do they waste their words."

15.9 The Master said, "The determined scholar and the man of virtue will not seek life at cost of injuring their virtue. They will even sacrifice their lives to fulfil virtue."

15.10 Zigong asked about the practice of virtue. The Master said, "A workman who wishes to do his work well, must first sharpen his tools. In whatever state you dwell, serve the most worthy among its officers, and make friends with the most virtuous among the scholars."

15.11 Yan Yuan asked about the governing of a state.

冕，樂則《韶》《舞》。放鄭聲，遠佞人。鄭聲淫，佞人殆。”

【譯文】顏淵問怎樣治理國家。孔子說：“用夏朝的曆法，（它符合季節規律。）乘殷朝的車子，（它簡樸。）戴周朝的禮帽，（它華麗。）音樂就用舜的《韶》和武王的《武》。捨棄鄭國的樂曲，遠離花言巧語諂媚的人。因為鄭國樂曲淫蕩，花言巧語諂媚的人危險。”

15·12 子曰：“人無遠慮，必有近憂。”

【譯文】孔子說：“一個人沒有長遠的考慮，便一定有眼前的憂患。”

15·13 子曰：“已矣乎！吾未見好德如好色者也。”

【譯文】孔子說：“算了吧！我沒有見過愛好美德像喜愛美貌一樣的人。”

15·14 子曰：“臧文仲其竊位者與！知柳下惠之賢而不與立也。”

【譯文】孔子說：“臧文仲大概是個做官而不幹事的人吧？他明知道柳下惠賢能，卻不給他職位。”

15·15 子曰：“躬自厚而薄責於人，則遠怨矣。”

【譯文】孔子說：“多責備自己，而少責備別人，就不致招來怨恨了。”

15·16 子曰：“不曰‘如之何，如之何’者，吾末如之何也已矣。”

【譯文】孔子說：“一個人不想想怎麼辦、怎麼辦的，我也拿他不知道怎麼辦才好。”

The Master said, "Follow the seasons of Xia; drive in a chariot of Yin; wear the ceremonial cap of Zhou; choose for music the Shao and its dance. Banish the tunes of Zhen, and keep far from men of glib tongue. The tunes of Zhen are licentious, men of glib tongue are dangerous."

15. 12 The Master said, "If a man takes no thought about what is far off, he will find troubles near at hand."

15. 13 The Master said, "Alas! I have not seen one who loves virtue as he loves beauty!"

15. 14 The Master said, "Did not Zang Wen Zhong steal his post? He knew the virtue and the talents of Liuxia Hui, and yet did not recommend Liuxia Hui for standing with him in court."

15. 15 The Master said, "He who demands much from himself and little from others, will keep himself from resentment."

15. 16 The Master said, "When a man does not continually ask himself 'what am I to do about this? What am I to do about this?', I really do not know what I am to do about him!"

15·17　子曰：“群居終日，言不及義，好行小慧，難矣哉！”

【譯文】孔子說：“大家整天在一起，說話沒有道理，喜歡賣弄小聰明，這種人很難有出息啊！”

15·18　子曰：“君子義以爲質，禮以行之，孫以出之，信以成之。君子哉！”

【譯文】孔子說：“君子以義為原則，用禮儀去實行，用謙遜的語言來說出它，用誠實的態度完成它，這真是一位君子啊！”

15·19　子曰：“君子病無能焉，不病人之不己知也。”

【譯文】孔子說：“君子只擔心自己沒有能力，不擔心別人不知道自己。”

15·20　子曰：“君子疾没世而名不稱焉。”

【譯文】孔子說：“君子擔心死後而名聲還不被別人稱頌。”

15·21　子曰：“君子求諸己，小人求諸人。”

【譯文】孔子說：“君子要求自己，小人要求別人。”

15·22　子曰：“君子矜而不爭，群而不黨。”

【譯文】孔子說：“君子莊矜而不爭執，合群而不鬧宗派。”

15·23　子曰：“君子不以言舉人，不以人廢言。”

【譯文】孔子說：“君子不因別人話說得好聽便提拔他，不因為別人品德不好而廢棄正確的話。”

15·24　子貢問曰：“有一言而可以終身行之者乎？”子曰：

15. 17 The Master said, "Those who spend a whole day together without any talk of righteousness and are fond of showing off their small smartness are difficult to instruct."

15. 18 The Master said, "A superior man in everything takes righteousness as his principle. He puts it into practice according to the rules of propriety, speaks it out with modesty and accomplishes it with sincerity. This is indeed a superior man."

15. 19 The Master said, "A superior man is distressed by his own want of ability. He is not distressed by others' not knowing him."

15. 20 The Master said, "A superior man worrys lest he make no reputation for himself when his life is done."

15. 21 The Master said, "A superior man makes demands upon himself; a small man makes demands upon others."

15. 22 The Master said, "A superior man is dignified, not quarrelsome; sociable, not a partisan."

15. 23 The Master said, "A superior man does not promote a man simply for his words; nor does he reject his good words because of the man."

15. 24 Zigong asked, "Is there any single saying that one

“其恕乎！己所不欲，勿施於人。”

【譯文】子貢問道：“有沒有一句可以畢生奉行的話呢？”孔子說：“大概是‘恕’吧！自己所不想要的，不要加在別人身上。”

15·25 子曰：“吾之於人也，誰毀誰譽？如有所譽者，其有所試矣。斯民也，三代之所以直道而行也。”

【譯文】孔子說：“我對於別人，詆毀了誰？稱贊了誰？如果我有所稱贊，是經過了考驗的。夏、商、周三代的人都如此，所以他們都能走正直的道路。”

15·26 子曰：“吾猶及史之闕文也。有馬者借人乘之，今亡矣夫！”

【譯文】孔子說：“我還能夠看到史書中存疑的地方。有馬的人，先藉給別人使用，今天卻沒有這種人了。”

15·27 子曰：“巧言亂德。小不忍，則亂大謀。”

【譯文】孔子說：“花言巧語敗壞道德。小事情不能忍耐，就會敗壞大事情。”

15·28 子曰：“衆惡之，必察焉；衆好之，必察焉。”

【譯文】孔子說：“大家都厭惡他，一定要考察一下；大家都喜歡他，一定要考察一下。”

15·29 子曰：“人能弘道，非道弘人。”

【譯文】孔子說：“人能夠把‘道’發揚光大，不是‘道’能夠把人發揚光大。”

15·30 子曰：“過而不改，是謂過矣。”

can act upon for all one's life?"The Master said, "Conscientiousness to others (Shu), perhaps. What you do not want done to yourself, do not do to others."

15. 25 The Master said, "In my dealings with men, whom do I blame? Whom do I praize? Or if I do praise anybody, it is after trial. Because of these people the three dynasties pursued the path of straightforwardness."

15. 26 The Master said, "I can still see blank spaces in history books. An owner of a horse would lend him to others to ride. Today there are no such things!"

15. 27 The Master said, "Clever talk confounds virtue; impatience of trifles confounds great projects."

15. 28 The Master said, "When everyone hates a man, it is necessary to examine into the case; when everyone loves a man, it is necessary to examine into the case."

15. 29 The Master said, "A man can enlarge the Way; but there is no Way that can enlarge a man."

15. 30 The Master said, "To have faults and not to cor-

【譯文】孔子說："錯了卻不改正，這就叫錯誤了。"

15·31 子曰："吾嘗終日不食，終夜不寢，以思，無益，不如學也。"

【譯文】孔子說："我曾經整日不吃，整夜不睡，去冥思苦想，沒有什麽益處，還不如去學習。"

15·32 子曰："君子謀道不謀食。耕也，餒在其中矣；學也，祿在其中矣。君子憂道不憂貧。"

【譯文】孔子說："君子謀求學問，不謀求衣食。耕田要餓肚皮；學習可以得到俸祿。君子擔憂得不到學問，不擔憂貧窮。"

15·33 子曰："知及之，仁不能守之；雖得之，必失之。知及之，仁能守之。不莊以涖之，則民不敬。知及之，仁能守之，莊以涖之，動之不以禮，未善也。"

【譯文】孔子說："靠聰明才智得到了官職，不用仁德保持它，縱然得到了，一定會喪失。靠聰明才智得到了官職，用仁德保持它，如果不莊重嚴肅地治理百姓，百姓就不會恭恭敬敬。靠聰明才智得到了官職，用仁德保持它，莊重嚴肅地治理百姓，如果不用禮法去動員百姓，那也是不完善的。"

15·34 子曰："君子不可小知而可大受也，小人不可大受而可小知也。"

【譯文】孔子說："君子不可以用小事去考驗他，卻可以承擔重大任務；小人不可以承擔重大任務，卻可以用小事去考驗他。"

15·35 子曰："民之於仁也，甚於水火。水火，吾見蹈而死

rect them,---this,indeed,is to have faults."

15. 31 The Master said,"I once spent in thinking the whole day without food and the whole night without sleep. It was no use. To learn is better."

15. 32 The Master said,"A superior man aims at truth; he does not aim at food. Ploughing may end in famine;learning may end in rank and pay. But a superior man is anxious lest he should not get truth; he is not anxious lest poverty should come upon him."

15. 33 The Master said,"When a man's wisdom is sufficient to bring him into power,if his virtue is not sufficient to enable him to hold,though he gets it,he will lose again. When his wisdom is sufficient to bring him into power,and he has virtue enough to hold it fast,if he cannot govern with dignity, the people will not respect him. When his wisdom is sufficient to bring him into power,he has virtue enough to hold it fast, and he governs also with dignity,yet if he does not rule the people according to the rules of propriety,full excellence is not reached."

15. 34 The Master said,"A superior man cannot be known in small matters,but he may be entrusted with great responsibilities. The small man may not be entrusted with great responsibilities,but he may be known in small matters."

15. 35 The Master said,"Virtue is more to the people than fire and water. I have seen men die from treading fire and water, but I have never seen a man die from treading on

者矣,未見蹈仁而死者也。”

【譯文】孔子說:“百姓需要仁德,勝過需要水火。水和火,我看見有人投入到那裏面去而死了的,卻没見過踐行仁德而死了的。”

15·36 子曰:“當仁,不讓於師。”

【譯文】孔子說:“面對着仁德的事情,對老師也不謙讓。”

15·37 子曰:“君子貞而不諒。”

【譯文】孔子說:“君子講究大信用,不講究小信用。”

15·38 子曰:“事君,敬其事而後其食。”

【譯文】孔子說:“事奉君主,嚴肅認真地工作,把俸禄的事放在後面。”

15·39 子曰:“有教無類。”

【譯文】孔子說:“人人我都進行教育,没有任何區别。”

15·40 子曰:“道不同,不相爲謀。”

【譯文】孔子說:“主張不同,不互相商量問題。”

15·41 子曰:“辭達而已矣。”

【譯文】孔子說:“言辭能夠表達意思就行了。”

15·42 師冕見,及階,子曰:“階也。”及席,子曰:“席也。”皆坐,子告之曰:“某在斯,某在斯。”

師冕出。子張問曰:“與師言之道與?”子曰:“然;固相師之道也。”

virtue."

15.36 The Master said, "When it comes to virtue, one need not avoid competing with one's teacher."

15.37 The Master said, "From a superior man consistency is expected, but not blind fidelity."

15.38 The Master said, "In serving his prince, one should be intent upon work, not bent upon the pay."

15.39 The Master said, "There is no distinction of castes in instruction."

15.40 The Master said, "Those who follow a different Way cannot take counsel together."

15.41 The Master said, "In speeches all that matters is to convey the meaning."

15.42 The music-master Mian[①] came to visit Confucius. When they reached the steps, the Master said, "Here are the steps." When they reach the mat, the Master said, "Here is the

① The man being blind, like most musicians in the East.

【譯文】一位叫冕的樂師來進見孔子，走到臺階邊，孔子說："這是臺階。"到了坐席前，又說："這是坐席。"都坐定了，(因為樂師冕是瞎子，)孔子告訴他說："我在這裏，我在這裏。"

師冕出來了。子張問："這是和樂師談話的方法嗎?"孔子說："對，這是幫助樂師的方法。"

季氏篇第十六

16·1 季氏將伐顓臾。冉有、季路見於孔子曰："季氏將有事於顓臾。"

孔子曰："求！無乃爾是過與？夫顓臾，昔者先王以爲東蒙主，且在邦域之中矣，是社稷之臣也。何以伐爲？"

冉有曰："夫子欲之，吾二臣者皆不欲也。"

孔子曰："求！周任有言曰：'陳力就列，不能者止。'危而不持，顚而不扶，則將焉用彼相矣？且爾言過矣，虎兕出於柙，龜玉毁於櫝中，是誰之過與？"

冉有曰："今夫顓臾，固而近於費。今不取，後世必爲子孫憂。"

孔子曰："求！君子疾夫舍曰欲之而必爲之辭。丘也聞有國有家者，不患寡當作貧而患不均，不患貧當作寡而患不安。蓋均無貧，和無寡，安無傾。夫如是，故遠人不服，則修文德以來之。既來之，則安之。今由與求也，相夫子，遠人不服，而不能來也；邦分崩離析，而不能守也；而謀動干戈於邦内。吾恐季孫之憂，不在顓臾，而在蕭牆之内也。"

【譯文】季氏準備攻打顓臾。冉有、子路去見孔子，說："季氏準備對顓臾使用武力。"

mat. "When all were seated, the Master told him, "So-and-so is here; so-and-so is here."

When the music-master had left, Zizhang said, "Is this the way to speak to a music-master?" The Master said, "Yes. This is surely the Way to help a music-master."

BOOK XVI JI SHI

16. 1 The Head of Ji family was going to attack Zhuanyu①. Ran You and Jilu②came to see Confucius and said, "The Head of the Ji family is going to use military forces against Zhuanyu."

Confucius said, "Qiu! is it not you who are in fault? Zhuanyu was long ago appointed by the former king to preside over the sacrifices to the Mount Dongmeng. Moreover, it lies within the boundaries of our state, and it is a vassal state of ours. Why are you going to attack it?"

Ran You said, "Our lord wishes it; neither of us two ministers wishes it."

The Master said, "Qiu, there are the words of Zhou Ren③, 'He who can put forth his ability takes his place in the ranks of office; he who cannot, retires from it.' Of what use is such a guide to a blind man, who sees him tottering, but does not support him, sees him falling, but does not prop him up?

---

① A small feudatory state within the borders of Lu.

② Zilu. He and Ran You were at the time in the service of the Ji family.

③ A ancient historiographer.

孔子說："冉求！這難道不應該責備你嗎？顓臾，上代君王曾經授權給他主持東蒙山的祭祀，而且那地方早已在魯國疆域之中，是魯國的臣屬，為什麼要去攻打它呢？"

冉有說："季孫要這麼幹，我們兩個都不同意。"

孔子說："冉求！周任有句話說：'獻出自己的力量，能夠做到的才去就職；不能，就不幹。'瞎子遇到危險，助手不去扶持；將要摔倒了，助手也不去攙扶，那又要助手幹什麼呢？你的話是錯了。老虎犀牛從籠子裏逃了出來，龜殼、美玉在匣子裏毀壞了，這是誰的過錯呢？"

冉有說："顓臾現在城牆很堅固，而且離季氏的封地費邑很近。現在不攻取下來，後世一定會給子孫留下禍害。"

孔子說："冉求！君子就討厭不說自己貪得無厭，卻一定另找托辭。我聽說過：無論諸侯或者大夫，不擔心貧窮，而擔心財富不平均；不擔心人口稀少，而擔心境內不安寧。因為財富平均，便無所謂貧窮；境內和睦團結，便不會覺得人口稀少；境內安寧，便不會覺得有傾覆的危險。如果這樣，遠方的人還不歸服，便修明仁義禮教使他們自動歸服。他們已經歸服了，就得使他們安心。現在仲由和冉求，你們輔助季氏，遠方的人不歸服，而不能使他們自動來歸；國家支離破碎，而不能保全住；反而要在國內動用武力。我擔心季孫的憂患不在顓臾，而在自己宮廷裏面。"

16·2 孔子曰："天下有道，則禮樂征伐自天子出；天下無道，則禮樂征伐自諸侯出。自諸侯出，蓋十世希不失矣；自大夫出，五世希不失矣；陪臣執國命，三世希不失矣。天下有道，則政

Moreover, your plea is a false one. When a tiger or a buffalo escapes from its cage, when a tortoise-shell or jade is broken in its box, whose fault is it?"

Ran You said, "Now Zhuanyu is strongly fortified and is close to Bei[1]; if it is not taken today, in days to come it will certainly bring trouble to our sons and grandsons."

Confucius said, "Qiu, a superior man hates the man who makes excuses instead of directly saying 'I want it'. I have heard that rulers of states and chiefs of families are not troubled about poverty, but are troubled about misapportionments; that they are not troubled lest their people should be few, but troubled lest they should be unstable. For, if all is well-apportioned, there will be no poverty; if they are in harmony, there will be no lack of men; if stability reigns, there will be no danger of collapse. If all these are done, and yet the people of far-off lands still do not submit, then the ruler should attract them by encouraging ritual and music. Once they have been attracted, they must be made contented and tranquil. Now, here are you, You and Qiu, assisting your lord, the people of far lands do not submit to him, and he cannot attract them to him. In his own state there are divisions and tottery, disruption and cleft, but he cannot save it. And yet he is planning to use military force within the borders of his own land. I am afraid that the troubles of the Ji family will not rise in Zhuanyu, they will rise within his own palace wall."

16. 2 The Master said, "When the Way prevails under

---

① The chief castle of the Ji family.

不在大夫。天下有道，則庶人不議。”

【譯文】孔子說：“天下政治清明，制禮作樂和出兵徵討由天子決定；天下腐敗黑暗，制禮作樂和出兵徵討由諸侯決定。由諸侯決定，大概傳到十代以後，他們很少有不喪失權柄的；由大夫決定，傳到五代以後，很少有不喪失權柄的；若是大夫的家臣把持國家大權，傳到三代便很少有不喪失的了。天下政治清明，國家最高政治權力不會由大夫把持。天下政治清明，百姓不會議論紛紛。”

16·3 孔子曰：“祿之去公室五世矣，政逮於大夫四世矣，故夫三桓之子孫微矣。”

【譯文】孔子說：“魯國政權離開魯君已經有五代了；政權落到卿大夫手中已經有四代了，所以桓公的三房子孫也衰微了。”

16·4 孔子曰：“益者三友，損者三友。友直，友諒，友多聞，益矣。友便辟，友善柔，友便佞，損矣。”

【譯文】孔子說：“有益的朋友有三種，有害的朋友也有三種。和正直的人交朋友，和誠實的人交朋友，和見聞廣博的人交朋友，便受益了。和逢迎諂媚的人交朋友，和當面恭維、背後毀謗的人交朋友，和誇誇其談、華而不實的人交朋友，便有害了。”

16·5 孔子曰：“益者三樂，損者三樂。樂節禮樂，樂道人之善，樂多賢友，益矣。樂驕樂，樂佚遊，樂晏樂，損矣。”

【譯文】孔子說：“有益的樂趣有三種，有害的樂趣也有三種。以得到禮樂的調節為快樂，以宣揚別人的好處為快樂，以交了不少賢明人物為快樂，這就受益了。以驕奢淫逸為快樂，以遊

Heaven, all orders concerning ceremonies, music and punitive expeditions are issued by the Son of Heaven (emperor). When the Way does not prevail, such orders are issued by the feudal princes. When such orders are issued by the feudal princes, the dynasty will rarely last for ten generations. When they are issued by the state ministers, the dynasty will rarely last for five generations. When the retainers of the great officers sway a state's fate, the dynasty will rarely last for three generations. When the Way prevails under Heaven, power does not lie with ministers. When the Way prevails under Heaven, the common people do not keep on talking about public affairs."

16. 3 Confucius said, "The state power has left the ducal house of Lu for five generations; the government has been in the hands of the great officers for four generations. On this account, the descendants of the Three Huan[1] are fast declining."

16. 4 Confucius said, "There are three sorts of friends which are advantageous, and three which are harmful. Friendship with the upright; friendship with the sincere; friendship with those who have heard much: ——these are advantageous. Friendship with the fawning; friendship with the insinuatingly soft; friendship with the glib-tongued: ——these are harmful."

16. 5 Confucius said, "There are three sorts of pleasures which are advantageous, and three which are harmful. The pleasure in being adjusted by ritual and music; the pleasure in speaking of the good of others; and the pleasure in having worthy friends: ---these pleasures are advantageous. The pleasure

---

① The three families, Meng, Shu, and Ji.

蕩忘返為快樂，以聚衆大吃大喝為快樂，便有害了。”

16·6 孔子曰:“侍於君子有三愆:言未及之而言謂之躁,言及之而不言謂之隱,未見顔色而言謂之瞽。”

【譯文】孔子說:“陪侍君子容易犯三種過失:不該他說話時卻急於先說,叫做急躁;該他說時卻不開口叫做隱瞞;不看別人的臉色便貿然開口,叫做瞎了眼睛。”

16·7 孔子曰:“君子有三戒:少之時,血氣未定,戒之在色;及其壯也,血氣方剛,戒之在鬬;及其老也,血氣既衰,戒之在得。”

【譯文】孔子說:“君子有三件應該警惕戒備的事:年輕的時候,血氣還沒有穩定,警戒自己不要迷戀女色;到了壯年,血氣正旺盛,警戒自己不要逞強相鬬;等到老了,血氣已經衰弱,警戒自己不要貪得無厭。”

16·8 子曰:“君子有三畏:畏天命,畏大人,畏聖人之言。小人不知天命而不畏也,狎大人,侮聖人之言。”

【譯文】孔子說:“君子懼怕三件事:懼怕天命,懼怕權貴人物,懼怕聖人的言論。小人不懂得天命,因而不懼怕,褻瀆權貴人物,侮慢聖人的言論。”

16·9 孔子曰:“生而知之者上也,學而知之者次也;困而學之,又其次也;困而不學,民斯爲下矣。”

【譯文】孔子說:“生下來就知道的人是上等;學了才知道的人是次等;遇到困難不得不學的人又次一等;遇到困難而不學習,這種人是最下等的了。”

in profligate enjoyments; the pleasure in idle gadding about; the pleasure in the joys of feasting:---these pleasures are harmful."

16.6 Confucius said, "There are three mistakes that are liable to be made when waiting upon a superior man. To speak before the time has come, this is called rashness. Not to speak when the time has come, this is called concealment. To speak without first looking at the countenance of the superior man, this is called blindness."

16.7 Confucius said, "There are three things which the superior man guards against. In youth, when the physical powers are not yet settled, he guards against lust. In his prime of life, when the physical powers are full of vigour, he guards against strife. In old age, when the physical powers are decaying, he guards against greed."

16.8 Confucius said, "There are three things of which a superior man is in awe. He is in awe of the will of Heaven. He is in awe of great men. He is in awe of the words of sages. The small man does not know the will of Heaven and so he does not stand in awe of it. He is disrespectful to great men. He scoffs at the words of sages."

16.9 Confucius said, "Highest are those who are born with innate knowledge. Next are those who get possession of knowledge by learning. After them come those who start learning only when they feel puzzled. As to those who do not learn even when they feel puzzled, they are the lowest of the people."

16·10 孔子曰:"君子有九思:視思明,聽思聰,色思溫,貌思恭,言思忠,事思敬,疑思問,忿思難,見得思義。"

【譯文】孔子說:"君子有九種事情需要考慮:看要考慮看明白了嗎;聽要考慮聽清楚了嗎;臉色要考慮溫和嗎;容貌要考慮恭敬嗎;言語要考慮忠實嗎;工作要考慮認真嗎;疑惑要考慮怎樣去提問;憤怒要考慮會不會有後患;遇見有所得,要考慮是否該得。"

16·11 孔子曰:"見善如不及,見不善如探湯。吾見其人矣,吾聞其語矣。隱居以求其志,行義以達其道。吾聞其語矣,未見其人也。"

【譯文】孔子說:"看見善良的,努力追求,好像唯恐趕不上似的;看見邪惡,盡力避開,好像手將伸進沸水裏。我遇見過這樣的人,也聽到過這樣的話。避世隱居來保全自己的志向,做合乎正義的事來貫徹自己的主張。我聽過這樣的話,卻没有遇見過這樣的人。"

16·12 齊景公有馬千駟,死之日,民無德而稱焉。伯夷、叔齊餓于首陽之下,民到于今稱之。其斯之謂與?

【譯文】齊景公有馬四千匹,到他死的時候,百姓都認為他没有什麼德行值得稱贊的。伯夷、叔齊餓死在首陽山下,百姓到今天還稱贊他們。大概說的就是這個意思吧?

16·13 陳亢問於伯魚曰:"子亦有異聞乎?"

對曰:"未也。嘗獨立,鯉趨而過庭。曰:'學《詩》乎?'對曰:'未也。''不學《詩》,無以言。'鯉退而學《詩》。他日,又獨立,鯉趨而過庭。曰:"學禮乎?'對曰:'未也。''不學禮,無以立。'鯉退而學禮。聞斯二者。"

16. 10 Confucius said, "A superior man has nine cares. In seeing he is careful to see clearly; in hearing he is careful to hear distinctly; in his countenance he is careful to be benign; in his manner to be respectful; in his words to be sincere; in his work to be diligent. When in doubt he is careful to ask others; when he is angry he has a care for the consequences, and when he sees gain to be got, he thinks of righteousness."

16. 11 Confucius said, "When seeing good, they pursue it, as if they could not reach it; when seeing evil, they shrink from it, as they would from putting the hand into boiling water: --- I have seen such men. I have heard such words. By dwelling in seclusion they seek the fulfilment of their aims; by practising righteousness they carry out their principles: --- I have heard these words, but I have not seen such men."

16. 12 Duke Jing of Qi had a thousand teams of horses, but on the day of his death, the people could think of no single virtue for which to praise him. Boyi and Shuqi died of hunger at the foot of Shouyang Mountain, yet the people praise them down to this very day. Is not the saying illustrated by this?①

16. 13 Cheng Kang② asked Boyu③, "Have you heard any lessons different from what we have heard?"

Boyu replied, "No. Once when he was standing alone and I was hurrying past him across the court-yard, he said to me, 'Have you learned poems?' I answered, 'No.' 'If you don't

---

① Some words lacked here, or this sentence was out of place.

② i. e. zi Qin.

③ Kong Li, Confucius's son.

陳亢退而喜曰:“問一得三,聞《詩》,聞禮,又聞君子之遠其子也。”

【譯文】陳亢向(孔子的兒子)伯魚問道:“您在老師那裏得到不同於一般人的教授嗎?”

伯魚回答說:“没有。他曾經獨自站着,我快步走過庭中。他說:‘學過《詩》嗎?’我回答說:‘没有。’他說:‘不學《詩》,就不善於說話。’我退回來就學《詩》。另一天,他又獨自站着,我又快步地走過庭中。他說:‘學了禮嗎?’我回答說:‘没有。’他說:‘不學禮,便在社會上無法站穩脚跟。’我回來便去學禮。我只聽到這兩件事。”

陳亢回去高興地說:“問一件事,知道了三件事。聽到學《詩》,聽到學禮,還聽到君子不偏愛自己的兒子。”

16·14 邦君之妻,君稱之曰夫人,夫人自稱曰小童;邦人稱之曰君夫人,稱諸異邦曰寡小君,異邦人稱之亦曰君夫人。

【譯文】國君的妻子,國君稱她為夫人,她稱自己為小童;本國人稱她為君夫人,對外國人便稱她為寡小君,外國人也稱她為君夫人。

陽貨篇第十七

17·1 陽貨欲見孔子,孔子不見,歸孔子豚。

孔子時其亡也,而往拜之。

遇諸塗。

謂孔子曰:“來!予與爾言。”曰:“懷其寶而迷其邦,可謂仁乎?”曰:“不可。好從事而亟失時,可謂知乎?”曰:“不可。日月逝矣,歲不我與。”

孔子曰:“諾,吾將仕矣。”

study poems, you will have no holds on words.' So I retired and learned the poems. Another day he was standing alone, and as I hurried across the court-yard, he said to me, 'Have you studied the rules of propriety?' I answered, 'No.' 'If you don't study the rules of propriety,' he said, 'you can't take your stand.' I then retired and studied the rules of propriety. These two things I have heard from him."

Cheng Kong went away delighted, saying, 'I asked one thing, but got three things. I have heard about poems. I have heard about the rules of propriety. I have also heard that the superior man keeps his son at a distance."

16. 14 The wife of the prince of a state is called by him Fu Ren. She calls herself Xiao Tong. The people of the state call her Jun Fu Ren, and to the people of other states, they call her Gụa Xiao Jun. The people of other states also call her Jun Fu Ren.

BOOK XVII YANG HUO

17. 1 Yang Huo① wanted Confucius to see him, but Confucius would not see him. He sent Confucius a sucking pig.

Confucius chose a time when he knew Yang Huo was not at home, and went to thank him.

Confucius met him, however, on the road.

He said to Confucius, "Come, I have something to say to you." He then said, "Can he be called benevolent, who keeps

① The all-powerful, unscrupulous retainer of Ji family.

【譯文】陽貨想要孔子去見他，孔子不去見，陽貨送孔子(一頭蒸熟了的)小豬。

孔子探聽到他外出時去拜謝他。

在路上碰到了。

陽貨對孔子說："來！我和你說話。"陽貨說："懷有一身本領，卻聽任國家一蹋糊塗，可以叫做仁嗎？"他自己接着說："不可以。""一個人喜歡做事情，卻屢屢錯過機會，可以叫做聰明嗎？"他接着說："不可以。時光一天天過去了，歲月不會等待我們。"

孔子這才說："好吧，我準備做官了。"

17·2 子曰："性相近也，習相遠也。"

【譯文】孔子說："人的本性本來互相接近，因為受不同環境習俗的熏陶便大不一樣。"

17·3 子曰："唯上知與下愚不移。"

【譯文】孔子說："只有頭等聰明人和極端愚蠢的人，才是改變不了的。"

17·4 子之武城，聞弦歌之聲。夫子莞爾而笑，曰："割鷄焉用牛刀？"

子游對曰："昔者偃也聞諸夫子曰：'君子學道則愛人，小人學道則易使也。'"

子曰："二三子！偃之言是也。前言戲之耳。"

【譯文】孔子到武城去，聽到彈琴唱歌的聲音。孔子微笑着說："殺鷄，哪裏用得着宰牛刀呢？(治理這小地方，用得着如此禮樂教化嗎？)"

子游回答說："以前我聽見老師說過：'君子學習了道理便有仁愛之心，小人學習了道理便容易聽使喚。'"

his talents in his bosom, and leaves his country to confusion?" He replied by himself, "Certainly not. Can he be called wise, who longs to be engaged in public employment, and yet time after time misses the opportunity to do so?" He went on saying, "Certainly not. The days and months are gliding by, the years do not wait for us."

Confucius said, "All right, I will go into office."

17.2 The Master said, "By nature, men are nearly alike; by practice, they get to be far apart."

17.3 The Master said, "It is only the very wisest and the very stupidest who cannot change."

17.4 When the Master came to Wucheng①, he heard the sound of stringed instruments and singing. With a gentle smile, he said, "Why use an ox-knife to kill a chicken?"

Ziyou replied, "Master, I remember once hearing you say that the man of high station who has studied the Way will love mankind; the common people who have studied the Way are easy to rule."

The Master said, "My disciples, Yan's② words are right.

---

① Where Ziyou was in command.

② Ziyou's personal name.

孔子說："你們聽着，言偃的話是對的。我剛才的話不過是跟他開玩笑罷了。"

17·5 公山弗擾以費畔，召，子欲往。

子路不説，曰："末之也，已，何必公山氏之之也？"

子曰："夫召我者，而豈徒哉？如有用我者，吾其爲東周乎？"

【譯文】公山弗擾盤踞着費邑圖謀造反，叫孔子去，孔子打算去。

子路不高興，說："没地方去便算了，為什麼一定要去公山氏那裏呢？"

孔子說："那個叫我去的人，難道是白白叫我去嗎？如果有人用我，我將使周文王、武王的德政在東方再度興起啊！"

17·6 子張問仁於孔子。孔子曰："能行五者於天下爲仁矣。"

"請問之。"曰："恭，寬，信，敏，惠。恭則不侮，寬則得衆，信則人任焉，敏則有功，惠則足以使人。"

【譯文】子張問孔子怎樣實行仁政。孔子說："能夠在普天之下實行五種品德的，便是仁德了。"

子張說："請教哪五種？"孔子說："莊重，寬厚，誠實，勤敏，慈惠。莊重就不會遭受侮辱，寬厚就會得到大衆的擁護，誠實就會得到別人的任用，勤敏工作就有成績，慈惠就能很好地使喚別人。"

17·7 佛肸召，子欲往。

子路曰："昔者由也聞諸夫子曰：'親於其身爲不善者，君子不入也。'佛肸以中牟畔，子之往也，如之何？"

子曰："然，有是言也。不曰堅乎，磨而不磷；不曰白乎，涅而

What I said just now was only meant as a joke."

17.5 Gongshan Furao[1], when he held Bei in rebellion, he sent for the Master, who was inclined to go.

Zilu was displeased, and said, "If you have no place to go, that is all right. Why must you go to see Gongshan?"

The Master said, "He has sent for me, can it be for nothing? If anyone were to use me, I believe I could make a 'Zhou in the east'."

17.6 Zizhang asked Confucius about perfect virtue. Confucius said, "He who could put five things into practice everywhere under Heaven would be a man of perfect virtue."

Zizhang said, "May I ask what they are?" Confucius said, "Gravity, open-heartedness, sincerity, earnestness and kindness. Gravity escapes insult; open-heartedness wins all; sincerity gains men's trust; earnestness brings success; kindness gets service from the people."

17.7 Bi Xi[2] summoned the Master, and he was inclined to go.

Zilu said, "Master, I have heard you say, 'When a man is in his own person doing what is evil, a superior man will not

---

① Warden of Bei, the chief stronghold of the Ji family.

② A Jin officer.

不緇。吾豈匏瓜也哉？焉能繫而不食？”

【譯文】佛肸叫孔子去，孔子打算去。

子路說：“從前我聽見老師說過：‘親自做壞事的人那里，君子是不去的。’如今佛肸盤踞中牟叛亂，您要去，怎麼說得過去呢？”

孔子說：“對，我有過這話。不是說堅固的東西，磨也磨不薄嗎？不是說白的東西，染也染不黑嗎？我難道是匏瓜嗎？哪能夠只被人懸挂着而不給人食用呢？”

17·8 子曰：“由也！女聞六言六蔽矣乎？”對曰：“未也。”

“居！吾語女。好仁不好學，其蔽也愚；好知不好學，其蔽也蕩；好信不好學，其蔽也賊；好直不好學，其蔽也絞；好勇不好學，其蔽也亂；好剛不好學，其蔽也狂。”

【譯文】孔子說：“仲由呀！你聽說過六種品德會帶來六種弊病嗎？”子路回答說：“沒有。”

孔子說：“坐下！我告訴你。愛好仁德，卻不喜好學問，它的弊病是容易被愚弄；愛耍聰明卻不喜好學問，它的弊病是放蕩不羈；喜好誠實卻不喜好學問，它的弊病是（容易被人利用）害了自己；喜愛直率卻不喜好學問，它的弊病是說話尖刻傷人；喜愛勇敢卻不喜好學問，它的弊病是搗亂闖禍；喜愛剛強卻不喜好學問，它的弊病是膽大妄為。”

17·9 子曰：“小子何莫學夫《詩》？《詩》，可以興，可以觀，可以群，可以怨。邇之事父，遠之事君；多識於鳥獸草木之名。”

【譯文】孔子說：“學生們為什麼不學習《詩》呢？學《詩》可以培養聯想力，可以提高觀察力，可以鍛煉合群性，可以學得諷刺方法。近可以運用其中的道理事奉父母，遠可以用來服事君主，而且可以多多認識一些鳥獸草木的名稱。”

enter his house. 'Bi Xi is holding Zhongmu in revolt. If you go to him, what shall be said?"

The Master said, "Yes, I did say so. But is it not said that, if a thing is really hard, no grinding can make it thin? Is it not said that, if a thing is really white, no steeping can make it black? Am I a bitter gourd? How can I be only fit to hang up but not to eat?"

17.8 The Master said, "ZhongYou, have you heard the six virtues to which six degenerations are attached?" You replied, "No."

The Master said, "Sit down and I will tell you. Love of human-heartedness without love of learning degenerates into silliness. Love of wisdom without love of learning degenerates into presumption. Love of honesty without love of learning degenerates into being easily used and harming oneself. Love of straightforwardness without love of learning degenerates into harshness. Love of courage without love of learning degenerates into turbulance. Love of firmness without love of learning degenerates into arrogance."

17.9 The Master said, "My disciples, why do you not study the Book of Poetry? The Odes will help you to stimulate the mind, to deepen the observantion. They can teach you the art of sociability and make you know how to demonstrate with your superiors. They may be used at home in the service of your parents; abroad, in the service of the prince. Moreover, they will widen your acquaintance with the names of birds, beasts, plants and trees."

17·10 子謂伯魚曰:"女爲《周南》、《召南》矣乎?人而不爲《周南》、《召南》,其猶正牆面而立也與?"

【譯文】孔子對伯魚説:"你研究過《詩》中《周南》、《召南》嗎?一個人不研究《周南》、《召南》,那好比把臉面對着牆壁站立着,(一步也不能前進。)"

17·11 子曰:"禮云禮云,玉帛云乎哉? 樂云樂云,鐘鼓云乎哉?"

【譯文】孔子説:"禮呀禮呀,僅僅是指玉帛等禮物説的嗎?樂呀樂呀,僅僅是指鐘鼓等樂器説的嗎?"

17·12 子曰:"色厲而内荏,譬諸小人,其猶穿窬之盜也與?"

【譯文】孔子説:"外表聲色嚴厲,而内心怯弱,若用壞人作比喻,大概像個挖洞跳牆的小偷吧?"

17·13 子曰:"鄉願,德之賊也。"

【譯文】孔子説:"好好先生,是敗壞道德的人。"

17·14 子曰:"道聽而塗説,德之棄也。"

【譯文】孔子説:"在路上聽到傳言就四處傳播,這是對道德的背棄。"

17·15 子曰:"鄙夫可與事君也與哉?其未得之也,患得之當作患不得之。既得之,患失之。苟患失之,無所不至矣。"

【譯文】孔子説:"鄙陋之人,難道可以和他一道事奉君主嗎?當他没有得到職位的時候,就怕得不到;已經得到了,又怕失去

17. 10 The Master said to Boyu, "Have you studied Zhou Nan and Shao Nan[1] yet? The man who has not studied Zhou Nan and Shao Nan is as though he stands with his face right against a wall!"

17. 11 The Master said, "Ritual, ritual! Are jade and silk all that is meant by ritual? Music, music! Are bells and drums all that is meant by music?"

17. 12 The Master said, "He who assumed an outward air of fierceness while inwardly weak, in comparison with the small man, is like a thief who crawls through a hole in the wall."

17. 13 The Master said, "The good careful people of the villages spoil the true virtue."

17. 14 The Master said, "To spread what you have heard on the way, is to abandon virtue."

17. 15 The Master said, "How can one serve the prince along with those mean creatures? While they have not got office, their anxiety is how to get it. When they have got it, their anxiety is how to avoid losing it. When they are anxious for

---

① The first two books of the Book of Poetry.

它。如果怕失去，就無所不用其極了。”

17·16 子曰:“古者民有三疾，今也或是之亡也。古之狂也肆，今之狂也蕩；古之矜也廉，今之矜也忿戾；古之愚也直，今之愚也詐而已矣。”

【譯文】孔子說:“古代有三種毛病，今天連這都沒有了。古代的狂人肆意直言，如今的狂人便放蕩不羈了；古代矜持自尊的人威不可犯，現在矜持自尊的人一味惱怒蠻横；古代愚笨的人還直率，現在愚笨的人只是欺詐罷了。”

17·17 子曰:“巧言令色，鮮矣仁。”

【譯文】孔子說:“花言巧語，一副討好的臉色，這種人，沒有多少仁德。”

17·18 子曰:“惡紫之奪朱也，惡鄭聲之亂雅樂也，惡利口之覆邦家者。”

【譯文】孔子說:“我厭惡紫色奪去了大紅色的光彩，厭惡鄭國的樂曲擾亂了典雅的樂曲，厭惡尖嘴利舌傾覆國家的人。”

17·19 子曰:“予欲無言。”子貢曰:“子如不言，則小子何述焉?”子曰:“天何言哉? 四時行焉，百物生焉，天何言哉?”

【譯文】孔子說:“我想不說什麼了。”子貢說:“您如果不說，那我們傳述什麼呢?”孔子說:“天說了什麼呢?四季照樣運行，百物照樣生長，天說了什麼呢?”

17·20 孺悲欲見孔子，孔子辭以疾。將命者出户，取瑟而歌，使之聞之。

【譯文】孺悲想要見孔子，孔子託詞有病不見。傳達的人剛出

losing it, there is no length to which they will not go."

17. 16 The Master said, "In old days, men had three failings, which have, perhaps, died out today. The impetuous of old days were impatient of small restraints; the impetuous today are utterly insubordinate. The stern dignity of old days were stiff and gravely reserved; the stern dignity today are touchy and quarrelsome. The simple men of old days were straightforward; the simple men today show themselves in sheer deceit."

17. 17 The Master said, "Honey words and flattering looks seldom speak of virtue."

17. 18 The Master said, "I hate to see purple taking away the lustre of red. I hate to see the songs of Zheng corrupting the count music. I hate those with their sharp mouths overthrow kingdoms."

17. 19 The Master said, "I'd like not to speak." Zigong said, "If you, Master, do not speak, what shall we, your disciples, have to record?" The Master said, "Does Heaven speak? The four seasons run their courses, and all things are continually being produced. Does Heaven speak?"

17. 20 Ru Bei① wanted to see Confucius. Confucius excused himself on the plea of sickness. But when the messenger was going out through the door, Confucius took up his Se and

① A person of Lu

房門，孔子拿起瑟邊彈邊唱，故意使孺悲聽到。

17·21 宰我問："三年之喪，期已久矣。君子三年不爲禮，禮必壞；三年不爲樂，樂必崩。舊穀既没，新穀既升，鑽燧改火，期可已矣。"

子曰："食夫稻，衣夫錦，於女安乎？"

曰："安。"

"女安，則爲之！夫君子之居喪，食旨不甘，聞樂不樂，居處不安，故不爲也。今女安，則爲之！"

宰我出。子曰："予之不仁也！子生三年，然後免於父母之懷。夫三年之喪，天下之通喪也，予也有三年之愛於其父母乎！"

【譯文】宰我問："父母死亡，守孝三年，時間太久了。君子三年不去實行禮儀，禮儀一定會被破壞；三年不去奏音樂，樂曲一定會荒廢。舊穀已經吃完了，新穀又已登場，取火的木頭輪換了一遍，喪期一年也就可以了。"

孔子說："父母死了不到三年便吃稻米飯，穿錦緞衣，你心裏安不安呢？"

宰我說："安。"

孔子說："你心安，你就去幹吧！君子在服喪期間，吃美食不覺得味道好，聽到好的樂曲不覺得快樂，居住坐立都不安，所以才不那樣做。現在你心安，你就去做吧！"

宰我出來後，孔子說："宰予真不仁啊！兒子生下三年，然後才脱離父母懷抱。服喪三年，是天下通行的喪禮，宰予從父母那裏難道没有得到三年懷抱的愛撫嗎？"

17·22 子曰："飽食終日，無所用心，難矣哉！不有博弈者乎？爲之，猶賢乎已。"

【譯文】孔子說："整天吃飽飯，不用一點心思，難得有出息

sang to it, in order that the messenger might hear him.

17.21 Zai Wo said, "Three years' mourning is too long. If a superior man suspends their practice of propriety for three years, the propriety will decay. If he makes no music for three years, music will certainly be ruined. Within a year, the old grain has already vanished, the new grain has sprung up; and the round of woods for the fire-drill is ended. Surely a year would be enongh."

The Master asked, "Would you then feel at ease in eating good rice and wearing silk brocades?"

Zai Wo said, "Quitc at casc."

The Master said, "If you can feel at ease, do it. But a superior man, when in mourning, does not enjoy pleasant food, nor does he derive pleasure from music. If he is comfortably lodged in his home, he does not fccl at casc cither. That is why he abstains from these things. But now you feel at ease, you may do it."

Zai Wo then went out, and the Master said, "A man without human-heartedness! Only when a child is three years old does he leave his parents' arms. The three years' mourning is the universal mourning under heaven. And Yu, did he not enjoy his parents' affection for three years?"

17.22 The Master said, "Bad it is when a man crams himself with food all day and has nothing to task the mind! Are there not games such as draughts? Playing them would still be

啊！不是有擲采、下棋的遊戲嗎？幹幹也比閑散着好。”

17·23 子路曰：“君子尚勇乎？”子曰：“君子義以爲上，君子有勇而無義爲亂，小人有勇而無義爲盜。”

【譯文】子路問道：“君子崇尚勇敢嗎？”孔子說：“君子認爲正義是頭等要緊的。君子只講勇敢不講正義就會造反作亂，小人只講勇敢不講正義就會做強盜。”

17·24 子貢曰：“君子亦有惡乎？”子曰：“有惡：惡稱人之惡者，惡居下流流字衍文而訕上者，惡勇而無禮者，惡果敢而窒者。”

曰：“賜也亦有惡乎？”“惡徼以爲知者，惡不孫以爲勇者，惡訐以爲直者。”

【譯文】子貢說：“君子也有憎惡的事嗎？”孔子說：“有憎惡的事：憎惡專說別人壞處的人，憎惡在下位而毀謗在上位的人，憎惡勇敢卻沒有禮貌的人，憎惡勇敢果斷卻頑固不化的人。”

又說：“端木賜！你也有憎惡的事嗎？”子貢說：“我憎惡偷取別人的成果卻自以爲聰明的人，憎惡毫不謙虛卻自以爲勇敢的人，憎惡攻擊別人的短處卻自以爲正直的人。”

17·25 子曰：“唯女子與小人爲難養也，近之則不孫，遠之則怨。”

【譯文】孔子說：“只有女子和小人難得和他們共處。親近了就會無禮，疏遠了就會怨恨。”

17·26 子曰：“年四十而見惡焉，其終也已。”

【譯文】孔子說：“到了四十歲還被人討厭，他這一生也就完了。”

better than doing nothing at all."

17. 23 Zilu asked, "Does a superior man esteem courage?" The Master said, "A superior man gives the first place to righteousness. If a superior man has courage but no righteousness, he will become turbulent. If a small man has courage but no righteousness, he will become a thief."

17. 24 Zigong said, "Does a superior man has his hatreds also?" The Master said, "He has his hatreds. He hates those who spread evil of others, He hates those who being in a low station slander their superiors. He hates those who have only courage but do not know the rules of propriety. He hates those who are forward and determined but stubborn."

He then asked, "Ci, do you also have hatreds?" Zigong answered, "I hate those who mistake spying for wisdom. I hate those who mistake want of modesty for courage. I hate those who mistake tale-bearing for honesty."

17. 25 The Master said, "Only women and small men are very hard to deal with. If you are close to them, they become unruly. If you keep them at a distance, they are discontented."

17. 26 The Master said, "When a man of forty is still disliked, it will be so till the end."

微子篇第十八

18·1 微子去之,箕子爲之奴,比干諫而死。孔子曰:"殷有三仁焉。"

【譯文】(殷紂王昏亂殘暴,胞兄)微子離開他,(叔叔)箕子做了奴隸,(叔叔)比干勸阻他被處死。孔子說:"殷朝有三位仁人。"

18·2 柳下惠爲士師,三黜。人曰:"子未可以去乎?"曰:"直道而事人,焉往而不三黜?枉道而事人,何必去父母之邦?"

【譯文】柳下惠擔任法官,多次地被撤職。有人對他說:"您不可以離開這裏嗎?"他說:"正直地事奉君主,到哪裏去而不多次被撤職呢?不正直地事奉君主,為什麼一定要離開祖國呢?"

18·3 齊景公待孔子曰:"若季氏,則吾不能;以季、孟之間待之。"曰:"吾老矣,不能用也。"孔子行。

【譯文】齊景公講到怎樣對待孔子,說:"像魯君對待季氏那樣,我就辦不到。我打算用次於季氏、高於孟氏的待遇來對待他。"後來又說:"我老了,沒有什麼作為了。"孔子便離開了齊國。

18·4 齊人歸女樂,季桓子受之,三日不朝,孔子行。

【譯文】齊國送來歌姬舞女,季桓子接受了,一連三天不上朝聽政,孔子離去了。

18·5 楚狂接輿歌而過孔子曰:"鳳兮鳳兮!何德之衰?往者不可諫,來者猶可追。已而,已而!今之從政者殆而!"

孔子下,欲與之言。趨而辟之,不得與之言。

【譯文】楚國狂人接輿唱着歌經過孔子車前,唱道:"鳳凰呀,

BOOK XVIII WEI ZI

18. 1 Wei Zi[1] fled from him (tyrant King Zhou). QiZi[2] became a slave to him. Bigan[3] remonstrated with him and was killed. Confucius said, "The Yin dynasty possessed these three men of virtue."

18. 2 When Liuxia Hui was chief criminal judge, he was three times dismissed. Someone said to him, "Why not leave the state?" He answered, "If I serve men in an upright way, where can I go and not be three times dismissed? If I choose to serve men in a crooked way, what necessity is there for me to leave my native state?"

18. 3 Duke Jing of Qi, speaking of how to treat Confucius, said, "I cannot treat him as the King of Lu did the head of the Ji family. I will treat him as though he ranked between the head of Ji and the Meng." He also said, "I am old, I cannot accomplish anything more." Confucius then left the state of Qi.

18. 4 The people of Qi sent to Lu a present of geisha girls. Ji Huan Zi[4] accepted them, for three days no court was held. Confucius then left Lu.

18. 5 Jie Yu,[5] the madman of Chu, passed by Confucius, singing and saying, "Oh phoenix, phoenix! How dwindled is

---

① King Zhou's step-brother.
② King Zhou's uncle.
③ King Zhou's uncle.
④ Ji Kong Zi's father, a high official of Lu.
⑤ A hermit.

鳳凰呀！為什麼德行這麼衰微？過去的已不能挽回，今後的還來得及改正。算了吧，算了吧！今天當政的人物太危險！”

孔子下車，想和他交談，他趕快避開，孔子沒法和他交談。

18·6′ 長沮、桀溺耦而耕，孔子過之，使子路問津焉。

長沮曰：“夫執輿者爲誰？”

子路曰：“爲孔丘。”

曰：“是魯孔丘與？”

曰：“是也。”

曰：“是知津矣。”

問於桀溺。

桀溺曰：“子爲誰？”

曰：“爲仲由。”

曰：“是魯孔丘之徒與？”

對曰：“然。”

曰：“滔滔者天下皆是也，而誰以易之？且而與其從辟人之士也，豈若從辟世之士哉？”耰而不輟。

子路行以告。

夫子憮然曰：“鳥獸不可與同群，吾非斯人之徒與而誰與？天下有道，丘不與易也。”

【譯文】長沮、桀溺兩人一起耕作，孔子經過那裏，叫子路下去詢問渡口在哪裏。

長沮說：“那駕車子的是誰？”

子路說：“是孔丘。”

他說：“是魯國的孔丘嗎？”

子路說：“是的。”

他便說：“他知道渡口在哪裏。”

子路又去問桀溺。

your virtue! As to the past, reproof is useless; but the future may be remedied. Desist, desist! Peril awaits those who now engage in government."

Confucius got down from his carriage and wanted to speak with him, but Jie Yu hastened away, so that Confucius could not talk with him.

18. 6 Changju and Jieni[1] were working together in the fields. Confucius happened to pass by them, and sent Zilu to enquire of the ford.

Changju asked, "who is he that holds the reins in the carriage?"

Zilu answered, "It is Kong Qiu."

"Is it Kong Qiu of Lu?" asked he.

"Yes," said Zilu.

Changju said, "He knows the ford."

Zilu then enquired of Jieni.

Jieni asked, "who are you, sir?"

He answered, "I am Zongyou."

"Are you the disciple of Kong Qiu of Lu?" asked Jieni.

"I am." Zilu replied.

Jieni then said to him, "Disorder, like a swelling flood, spreads everywrere, and with whom will you change it? Than follow one who merely flees from bad men, had you not better follow us who flee from the world?" With this he went on covering the seed.

Zilu went back and told the Master, who said disappoint-

---

① Two hermits.

桀溺說:“您是誰?”

子路說:“我是仲由。”

他說:“您是魯國孔丘的門徒嗎?”

子路回答說:“是的。”

他便說:“到處都是像洪水一樣惡濁的東西,你們能同誰去改變它呢?而且你與其跟着孔丘那種逃避壞人的人,為什麼不跟隨我們這些逃避現實的人呢?”一邊說,一邊不停地覆蓋種子。

子路回來報告孔子。

孔子失望地說:“我們不能和鳥獸相處,不同人群中的你們在一起,又同誰在一起呢?天下政治清明,我就不參與改革了。”

18·7 子路從而後,遇丈人,以杖荷蓧。

子路問曰:“子見夫子乎?”

丈人曰:“四體不勤,五穀不分。孰爲夫子?”植其杖而芸。

子路拱而立。

止子路宿,殺鷄爲黍而食之,見其二子焉。

明日,子路行以告。

子曰:“隱者也。”使子路反見之。至,則行矣。

子路曰:“不仕無義。長幼之節,不可廢也;君臣之義,如之何其廢之?欲潔其身,而亂大倫。君子之仕也,行其義也。道之不行,已知之矣。”

【譯文】子路跟隨着孔子,走在後面,遇見一個老人,用手杖挑着除草用的工具。

子路問道:“您看見我的老師嗎?”

老人說:“四肢不勞動,五谷不能分辨,誰是你的老師呢?”老人把手杖插進泥土中就鋤草去了。

子路拱着手恭敬地站立着。

老人留子路住宿,殺了鷄,做好黃米飯給子路吃,叫他兩個

edly,"We cannot herd with birds and beasts. If I do not associate with these people, with mankind, with whom shall I associate? If the Way prevailed under Heaven, I should not be trying to chang."

18. 7 Once when Zilu was following the Master, fell behind and met an old man carring a tool for weeding (across his shoulder) on a walking stick.

Zilu asked him,"Have you seen my master?"

The old man replied,"You do not toil with your four limbs, nor can you distinguish five kinds of grain; who is your master?" With this, he planted his walking stick in the ground and began weeding.

Zilu stood by with his hands pressed together.

The old man kept Zilu for the night. He killed a fowl, prepared millet, and feasted him. He also introduced Zilu to his two sons.

Next day Zilu went on his way and reported what had happened to the Master.

The Master said,"He is a recluse." and sent Zilu back to see him. But when he got to the place, he found the old man had gone.

兒子出來相見。

第二天，子路趕上孔子，報告了這件事。

孔子說："這是位隱士。"叫子路回去見他。等子路到原來的地方，他已經搬走了。

子路說："不出來作官是不合情理的。長幼間的禮節不可廢棄，君臣間的禮節又怎麼可以廢棄呢？想使自己清白，卻搞亂了君臣間的倫理關係。君子出來作官，為的是履行君臣之義。我們的主張行不通，早已知道了。"

18·8 逸民：伯夷、叔齊、虞仲、夷逸、朱張、柳下惠、少連。子曰："不降其志，不辱其身，伯夷、叔齊與！"謂"柳下惠、少連，降志辱身矣，言中倫，行中慮，其斯而已矣。"謂"虞仲、夷逸，隱居放言，身中清，廢中權。我則異於是，無可無不可。"

【譯文】被遺落的人才有伯夷、叔齊、虞仲、夷逸、朱張、柳下惠、少連。孔子說："不降低自己的志氣，不辱沒自己的身份，要算伯夷、叔齊吧！"又講到柳下惠、少連，說："降低自己的志氣，辱沒自己的身份，但說話合乎法度，行為經過考慮，不過就是這樣罷了。"談到虞仲、夷逸，說："逃世隱居，放膽直言。自身清廉，被廢棄也合乎權宜。我則和他們不一樣，沒有什麼可以，也沒有什麼不可以。"

18·9 大師摯適齊，亞飯干適楚，三飯繚適蔡，四飯缺適秦，鼓方叔入於河，播鼗武入於漢，少師陽、擊磬襄入於海。

【譯文】太師摯前往齊國，亞飯樂師干前往楚國，三飯樂師繚前往蔡國，四飯樂師缺前往秦國，擊鼓樂師方叔入居黃河之濱，搖小鼓樂師武逃居漢水之濱，少師陽和擊磬的樂師襄到海邊去了。

Zilu said, "Not to take office is not right. The relations between old and young may not be set aside, how can the duty that binds minister to prince be set aside? Wishing to maintain his personal purity, he flouts the great relationship. The reason why the superior man tries to go into politics, is because he holds this to be right, even though he is well aware that his principle cannot prevail."

18.8 The men who had retired to privacy from the world were Boyi, Shuqi, Yuxhong, Yiyi, Zhuzhang, Liuxia Hui and Shaolian. The Master said, "Those who would not bend their will, or bring humiliation upon themselves were Boyi and Shuqi. It may be said of Liuxia Hui and Shaolian, that they bend their wills, and bring humiliation upon themselves, but their words corresponded with moral principles, and their actions were after consideration, this and no more. It may be said of Yuzhong and Yiyi, that they lived in seclusion, but gave the rein to the tongue. They preserved their purity. Their retreat was timely. But I am different from all of them. I know not 'must' or 'must not'."

18.9 The grand music-master Zhi went to Qi; Gan, the master of the band at the second meal, went to Chu; Liao, the band-master at the third meal, went to Cai; Que, the band-master at the fourth meal, went to Qin. The drum-master Fangshu went the Yellow River; The hand-drum master Wu, went to the Han River; Yang, the assistant music-master and Xiang, the master of the stone-chimes went to an island in the sea.

18.10 The Duke of Zhou addressed his son the Duke of

18·10　周公謂魯公曰:“君子不施其親,不使大臣怨乎不以。故舊無大故,則不棄也。無求備於一人。”

【譯文】周公對他兒子魯公伯禽說:“君子不怠慢他的親族,不讓大臣抱怨未被信任,老臣舊友没有嚴重過失就不要抛弃他們,對一個人不要求全責備。”

18·11　周有八士:伯達、伯適、仲突、仲忽、叔夜、叔夏、季隨、季騧。

【譯文】周朝有八位有教養的人:伯達、伯適、仲突、仲忽、叔夜、叔夏、季隨、季騧。

子張篇第十九

19·1　子張曰:“士見危致命,見得思義,祭思敬,喪思哀,其可已矣。”

【譯文】子張說:“士遇到危險就獻出生命,看見有利可圖便考慮該得不該得,祭祀時考慮是否嚴肅認真,有喪事時考慮是否悲痛哀傷,那也就可以了。”

19·2　子張曰:“執德不弘,信道不篤,焉能爲有?焉能爲亡?”

【譯文】子張說:“遵守道德不堅決,信仰真理不忠誠,這種人,有他也可,没他也可。”

19·3　子夏之門人問交於子張。子張曰:“子夏云何?”

對曰:“子夏曰:‘可者與之,其不可者拒之。’”

子張曰:“異乎吾所聞:君子尊賢而容衆,嘉善而矜不能。我之大賢與,於人何所不容?我之不賢與,人將拒我,如之何其拒人

Lu, saying, "A virtuous prince does not discard his kinsmen, nor does he cause the great minister to repine at not being used. He does not dismiss any old ministers or friends, unless he has good cause. He asks perfection of no man."

18. 11 Zhou had eight virtuous men (Shi): Boda, Bokuo, Zhongtu, Zhonghu, Shuye, Shuxia, Jisui, and Jigua.

BOOK XIX ZI ZHANG

19. 1 Zizhang said, "The virtuous man (Shi), who on face of danger is ready to sacrifice his life, who in sight of gain thinks first of righteousness, who keeps reverence in heart when sacrificing, who keeps grief in mind when mourning—such a man is all right."

19. 2 Zizhang said, "When a man holds fast virtue, but without enlarging it, and believes in the Way, but without firm sincerity, can this kind of man be said to be, or be said not to be?"

19. 3 The disciples of Zixia asked Zizhang about the principles of association. Zizhang said, "What does Zixia say?"

They replied, "Zixia says, 'Associate with those who are worthy associating with, and put away from those who are not worth associating."

也?”

【譯文】子夏的學生問子張如何交朋友。子張說:“子夏說了些什么呢?”

子夏的學生回答說:“子夏說:‘可以交便和他交朋友,不可以交的便拒絕他。’”

子張說:“我所聽到的和這不同:君子尊敬賢人,而且容納衆人,稱贊好人,而且同情無能的人。我是大賢人,對別人有什么不能容納的呢?我是不賢的人,別人會拒絕我,我怎麼能拒絕別人呢?”

19·4 **子夏曰:“雖小道,必有可觀者焉;致遠恐泥,是以君子不爲也。”**

【譯文】子夏說:“雖然是小小的技藝,也一定有值得一顧的地方。但恐怕對遠大的事業有妨礙,所以君子不去幹。”

19·5 **子夏曰:“日知其所亡,月無忘其所能,可謂好學也已矣。”**

【譯文】子夏說:“每天知曉自己所不知道的,每月不忘記已經能夠掌握的,可以說是愛好學習了。”

19·6 **子夏曰:“博學而篤志,切問而近思,仁在其中矣。”**

【譯文】子夏說:“廣博地學習,而且志向專一不變;對未曾理解的事懇切地向人求教,而且考慮當前的問題,仁德便在這當中了。”

19·7 **子夏曰:“百工居肆以成其事,君子學以致其道。”**

【譯文】子夏說:“各業的工匠在作坊里來完成他們的工作,君子則通過學習來獲得真理。”

Zizhong said,"This is different from what I have learned. A superior man honours the talented and virtuous,and bears with all. He praises the good and pities the incompetent. If I am a man of great talents and virtue,whom could I not bear with?If I am a man without talents and virtue,men will put me away from them. Why should I push others away?"

19. 4 Zixia said,"Even the minor crafts have something worth being looked at. But they tend to prove a hindrance to lofty ideals. For that reason a superior man does not practise them."

19. 5 Zixia said,"He who from day to day learns something new,and from month to month does not forget what he has already learnt,may indeed be called fond of learning."

19. 6 Zixia said,"He who studies widely and with a firm aim,who inquires with earnestness,and reflects with self application comes to virtue."

19. 7 Zixia said,"The hundred apprentices live in their workshops in order to accomplish their works . A superior man studies in order to reach the Way."

19·8 子夏曰："小人之過也必文。"

【譯文】子夏說："小人有了過失，一定加以掩飾。"

19·9 子夏曰："君子有三變：望之儼然，即之也溫，聽其言也厲。"

【譯文】子夏說："對君子的印象有三種變化：遠遠望去，莊嚴可畏；向他接近，溫和可親；聽他的話，嚴厲不苟。"

19·10 子夏曰："君子信而後勞其民；未信，則以爲厲己也。信而後諫；未信，則以爲謗己也。"

【譯文】子夏說："君子必須得到信任以後才去使喚百姓；沒有得到信任，他們會認為你在折磨他們；得到信任才去規勸上級；沒有得到信任，上級會認為你在毀謗他。"

19·11 子夏曰："大德不踰閑，小德出入可也。"

【譯文】子夏說："在重大節操上不能超越界限，生活小節上稍有出入是可以的。"

19·12 子游曰："子夏之門人小子，當灑掃應對進退，則可矣，抑末也。本之則無，如之何？"

子夏聞之，曰："噫！言游過矣！君子之道，孰先傳焉？孰後倦焉？譬諸草木，區以別矣。君子之道，焉可誣也？有始有卒者，其惟聖人乎！"

【譯文】子游說："子夏的學生們做做灑水掃地、接待客人、應對進退的事情，那是可以的，但這些只是末節小事。在學術上他們卻沒有基礎，這怎麼行呢？"

子夏聽到了，說："唉！言游錯了！君子的學術哪些先傳授，哪些後講述呢？譬如草木，各種各類是應該區別開來，君子的學

19. 8 Zixia said, "The small men always gloss their faults."

19. 9 Zixia said, "A superior man undergoes three changes. Seen from afar he looks stern; when approached, he is mild; when heard speaking, he is incisive."

19. 10 Zixia said, "A superior man will not lay burdens on the people unless he has gained their trust, otherwisc the people will think that he is oppressing them. He will not remonstrate his prince unless he has gaincd his trust, othcrwisc the prince will think that he is slandering him."

19. 11 Zixia said, "One must not transgress the boundary-line in the main principles, but he may pass or repass it in the small trifles."

19. 12 Ziyou said, "The disciples of Zixia, in sprinkling and sweeping floors, in answering and replying, in advancing and receding, are all right. But these are minor matters. They are left ignorant of what is essential. But what can come of branches without root?"

When Zixia heard of this, he said, "Alas, Yan You is wrong. Of the ways of the superior man, which is to be delivered first, and which is to be idle about? As in the case of plants, they have to be separately treated according to their classes. How can the ways of a superior man be misrepresent-

術，怎麽可以歪曲呢？傳授學術有始有終的，大概只有聖人吧！”

19·13　子夏曰：“仕而優則學，學而優則仕。”

【譯文】子夏說：“官作好了，有餘力就學習；學習好了，有餘力就去作官。”

19·14　子游曰：“喪致乎哀而止。”

【譯文】子游說：“居喪時，充分表現了他心中的悲哀也就夠了。”

19·15　子游曰：“吾友張也爲難能也，然而未仁。”

【譯文】子游說：“我的朋友子張是難能可貴的，但還沒有做到仁。”

19·16　曾子曰：“堂堂乎張也，難與并爲仁矣。”

【譯文】曾子說：“子張的為人高不可攀，很難把別人一同帶入仁德的境界。”

19·17　曾子曰：“吾聞諸夫子：人未有自致者也，必也親喪乎！”

【譯文】曾子說：“我聽老師說過，人沒有把內心的真實感情表露出來的時候，如果有，一定在父母逝世的時候吧！”

19·18　曾子曰：“吾聞諸夫子：孟莊子之孝也，其他可能也；其不改父之臣與父之政，是難能也。”

【譯文】曾子說：“我聽老師說過：孟莊子的孝道，其他都可以做到。而他在職期間，留用他父親的僚屬，保持他父親的政治措施，這是不容易做到的。”

ed? It is the sage alone who can transmit knowledge from beginning to end!"

19.13 Zixia said, "The officer, after doing all his duty to the state, should devote his spare energy to study. The scholar, after completing his studying, should devote his spare energy to service of the state."

19.14 Ziyou said, "Mourning, having been carried to the utmost degree of grief, should go no further."

19.15 Ziyou said, "My friend Zizhang can do things that are hard to be done, but yet he is not perfectly virtuous (Ren)."

19.16 Zeng Zi said, "How imposing is the manner of Zizang! It is difficult with him to practise perfect virtue."

19.17 Zeng Zi said, "I once heard the Master said that men may not show what is in them to the full extent, and yet they will be found to do so when mourning for their parents."

19.18 Zeng Zi said, "I once heard the Master said that in all else we may rival the filial piety of Meng Zhuang Zi, but in his not changing his father's ministers, nor his father's mode of government, he is hard to rival."

19·19 孟氏使陽膚爲士師,問於曾子。曾子曰:“上失其道,民散久矣。如得其情,則哀矜而勿喜!”

【譯文】孟氏任命陽膚作法官,陽膚向曾子求教。曾子說:“在上位的人不依規矩行事,百姓的心早就渙散了。你如果能審出罪犯的真情,就應該可憐、同情他們,不要自鳴得意。”

19·20 子貢曰:“紂之不善,不如是之甚也。是以君子惡居下流,天下之惡皆歸焉。”

【譯文】子貢說:“商紂王的罪惡,不像傳說的那麼厲害。所以君子最怕沾着惡名,一沾惡名,天下什麼壞事都會集中在他身上。”

19·21 子貢曰:“君子之過也,如日月之食焉:過也,人皆見之;更也,人皆仰之。”

【譯文】子貢說:“君子的過失如同日蝕月蝕一樣:犯錯誤的時候,人人都能看得見;當改正的時候,人人都仰望着。”

19·22 衛公孫朝問於子貢曰:“仲尼焉學?”子貢曰:“文武之道,未墜於地,在人。賢者識其大者,不賢者識其小者。莫不有文武之道焉。夫子焉不學?而亦何常師之有?”

【譯文】衛國的公孫朝問子貢說:“仲尼的學問是從哪裏得來的?”子貢說:“周文王、武王的道術并沒有失傳,散在人間。賢能的人抓住大節,不賢能的人只抓住小節。沒有地方沒有文王、武王的道術。我的老師到哪裏不能學呢?又為什麼一定要有專門的老師傳授呢?”

19·23 叔孫武叔語大夫於朝曰:“子貢賢於仲尼。”

19. 19 The chief of the Meng family appointed Yang Fu[①] as chief criminal judge. Yang Fu consulted Zeng Zi. Zeng Zi said, "The rulers have failed in their duties, and the people have gone astray for a long time. When you have found out the truth of any crime, be sad and pity them, and do not feel joyful."

19. 20 Zigong said, "The wickedness of King Zhou was not as great as that name implies. Therefore, a superior man hates to dwell on low ground, where all the evil of the world will flow in upon him."

19. 21 Zigong said, "The faults of a superior man are like the eclipses of the sun and the moon. When he has his faults, all men see them; when he corrects his faults, all men look up to him."

19. 22 Gongsun Chao of Wei asked Zigong, "Where did Zhongni get his learning?" Zigong said, "The Way of King Wen and King Wu of Zhou have not fallen into ruin. They are to be found among men. Men of talents and virtue grasp the major principles of them, and men without such talents and virtue grasp the minor principles. So there is no one who does not possess the Way of Wen and Wu. From whom indeed did our Master not learn? What need had he for a fixed teacher?"

19. 23 Shusun Wushu[②], talking to some high officers at

---

① A disciple of Zeng Zi.

② A high official of Lu.

子服景伯以告子貢。

子貢曰："譬之宮牆，賜之牆也及肩，窺見室家之好。夫子之牆數仞，不得其門而入，不見宗廟之美，百官之富。得其門者或寡矣。夫子之云，不亦宜乎！"

【譯文】叔孫武叔在朝廷告訴大夫們說："子貢比他老師仲尼還要好。"

子服景伯把這話告訴了子貢。

子貢說："拿房屋的圍牆作比喻吧，我家的圍牆只齊肩膀，誰都可以望見房屋的美好。我老師的圍牆有幾丈高，人們找不着大門進去，就看不到他那宗廟的壯美，房舍的多種多樣。能夠找着大門進去的人或許不多吧。叔孫武叔他老人家那麼說，不也是很自然的嗎？"

19·24 叔孫武叔毀仲尼。子貢曰："無以爲也！仲尼不可毀也。他人之賢者，丘陵也，猶可踰也；仲尼，日月也，無得而踰焉。人雖欲自絶，其何傷於日月乎？多見其不知量也。"

【譯文】叔孫武叔毀謗仲尼。子貢說："不要這樣做！仲尼是毀謗不了的。別人的賢能好比小山，還可以超過；仲尼好比太陽和月亮一樣，是不能超過的。有人縱然想自絕於太陽、月亮，那對太陽、月亮又有什麼損害呢？只是看出他太不自量了。"

19·25 陳子禽謂子貢曰："子爲恭也，仲尼豈賢於子乎？"

子貢曰："君子一言以爲知，一言以爲不知，言不可不慎也。夫子之不可及也，猶天之不可階而升也。夫子之得邦家者，所謂立之斯立，道之斯行，綏之斯來，動之斯和。其生也榮，其死也哀，如之何其可及也？"

【譯文】陳子禽對子貢說："您對仲尼那麼恭敬，難道他比您強嗎？"

court, said, "Zigong is better than his master."

Zifu Jingbo told this to Zigong.

Zigong daid, "Let me take as the comparison the wall round a house. My wall only reaches to the shoulders. One may peep over it, and see the goodly home within. The Master's wall is several fathoms high. If one does not find the door and enter by it, he cannot see the beauty of the ancestral temple, nor the rich variety of houses. But I think that those who find the door are few. So it is small wonder that he should have spoken like that."

19. 24 Shusun Wushu decried Zhongni. Zigong said, "Don't do that. Zhongni cannot be decried. The talents and virtue of other men are like hillocks and mounds that can be overleaped. Zhongni is like the sun or the moon that it is impossible to step over. If a man cut himself from them, what harm can he do to the sun or the moon? It only shows that he does not know his own measure."

19. 25 Chen Ziqin said to Zigong, "You are too modest. How can Zhongni be said to be superior to you?"

Zigong said, "For one word a superior man may be set down as wise, and for one word he is deemed to be not wise. So we should be careful indeed about what we say. None can equal the Master, as heaven cannot be climbed up to by a ladder. Had the master ever been put in control of a state or of a great fam-

子貢說："君子說一句話可以表現他的聰明，也可以說一句話表現他不聰明，說話是不能不謹慎的。我的老師是不可趕上的，如同上天不能用梯子一級級地爬上去一樣。我的老師如果當上國家的君主，或得到采邑成為卿大夫，他要百姓在社會上站住腳跟，百姓便都自然站住腳跟；引導百姓前進，百姓自然都跟着前進；安撫百姓，百姓自然都會前來投奔；動員百姓，百姓自然會同心協力。他老人家生得光榮，死得可惜可悲，別人怎麼能趕得上呢？"

堯曰篇第二十

20·1 堯曰："咨！爾舜！天之曆數在爾躬，允執其中。四海困窮，天祿永終。"

舜亦以命禹。

【譯文】堯（禪位給舜的時候）說："嘖嘖！你這位舜呀！上天的大任已經落到你身上了，你要真誠地堅持正確的方針。如果天下的百姓都陷入困苦貧窮的境地，上天給你的祿位也就會永遠終止了。"

舜（禪位時），也這樣告誡禹。

曰："予小子履敢用玄牡，敢昭告于皇皇后帝：有罪不敢赦。帝臣不蔽，簡在帝心。朕躬有罪，無以萬方；萬方有罪，罪在朕躬。"

【譯文】（商湯時，遭逢大旱，湯向上天求雨，）說："我這小子履謹用黑色的牡牛作祭品，明白地稟告輝煌的天帝：有罪的人不敢赦免他。您臣僕的善惡我也不掩蓋，您心裏是曉得的。我本人有罪，不要牽連天下萬方；天下萬方有罪，都歸罪我一人。"

周有大賚，善人是富。"雖有周親，不如仁人。百姓有過，在予一人。"

ily, it would have been as is described in the words:---He raised them and they stand; he leads them on and they follow; he pacifies them and they come up to him; he stimulates them and they are harmonious. His life was glorious, his death was bitterly lamented. How can he ever be equalled?"

BOOK XX YAO YUE

20. 1 Yao said, "Oh! you, Shun, the heavenly order of succession now rest in your own person. Faithfully hold fast the golden mean. If there shall be distress and want within the four seas, your heavenly gift will pass for ever."

Shun also said the same words in giving his charge to Yu.

Tang[①] said, "I, your child Lü, venture to sacrifice a black ox, and veture to proclaim before you, O most great and sovereign God, that I dare not forgive the sinner, nor slay your servants. Oh God, you know all about this. If I in my person do any wrong, let it never be visited on the people of myriad regions. If in the myriad regions any wrong be done, let it be visited upon my person."

Zhou granted titles and territories, and the good were enriched. King Wu said, "Although I have my own kinsmen, they are less to me than the virtuous. If the people do wrong, let the

① Founder of the Yin dynasty, when praying Heaven for rain.

【譯文】周朝大加封賞，使善良的人都富貴起來。周武王說："我雖然有至親，不如有仁德之人。百姓有過錯，由我一人來承擔。"

謹權量，審法度，修廢官，四方之政行焉。興滅國，繼絶世，舉逸民，天下之民歸心焉。

【譯文】謹慎地檢查度量衡，審訂禮樂制度，恢復已廢棄的官職，全國政令就會通行了。恢復被滅亡的國家，接續已斷絶的世族，選拔被遺落的人才，天下的百姓就都會心悦誠服。

所重：民、食、喪、祭。

【譯文】所重視的是：人民、糧食、喪禮、祭祀。

寬則得衆，信則民任焉，敏則有功，公則説。

【譯文】寬厚就會得到衆人的擁護，誠信就會得到别人的任用，勤快就會有功績，公平就會使百姓高興。

20·2 子張問於孔子曰："何如斯可以從政矣？"

子曰："尊五美，屏四惡，斯可以從政矣。"

子張曰："何謂五美？"

子曰："君子惠而不費，勞而不怨，欲而不貪，泰而不驕，威而不猛。"

子張曰："何謂惠而不費？"

子曰："因民之所利而利之，斯不亦惠而不費乎？擇可勞而勞之，又誰怨？欲仁而得仁，又焉貪？君子無衆寡，無小大，無敢慢，斯不亦泰而不驕乎？君子正其衣冠，尊其瞻視，儼然人望而畏之，斯不亦威而不猛乎？"

子張曰："何謂四惡？"

子曰："不教而殺謂之虐；不戒視成謂之暴；慢令致期謂之賊；猶之與人也，出納之吝謂之有司。"

【譯文】子張問孔子説："怎樣才可以治理政事呢？"

blame be thrown upon me alone."

Attend to weights and measures, revise the system ritual, restore the discarded offices, thus order will reign on all sides. Revive states that had been destroyed, re-establish lines of succession that had been broken, and call to office those who had been neglected, then all hearts of the people under Heaven will turn to him.

What the greatest attention should be paid to were the people, the food, the rites of mourning and sacrifice.

Generosity wins all; sincerity wins the people's trust; diligence brings the success; and justice delights all.

20. 2 Zizhang asked Confucius, "What must a man do that he may conduct government properly?"

The Master said. "He. who esteems the five virtues, and avoid the four vices, may conduct government properly."

Zizhang said, "What are the five virtues?"

The Master said, "A superior man is benevolent without great expenditure; he lays tasks on the people without arousing their resentment; he has desires without being covetous; he maintains a dignified ease without being proud; he inspires awe without being fierce."

Zizhang said, "What is meant by being benevolent without great expenditure?"

The Master said, "If he makes more beneficial to the people the things from which they natually derive benifit, is he not benevolent without great expenditure? If he imposes upon them

孔子說："尊崇五種美德，排除四種惡政，這就可以治理政事了。"

子張說："什麼是五種美德？"

孔子說："君子給人民好處，自己卻不耗費；使喚百姓，百姓卻不怨恨；自己有所求，卻不貪婪；安寧矜持卻不驕傲；有威嚴卻不兇猛。"

子張說："什麼是給人民好處，而自己卻不耗費？"

孔子說："凡百姓能得到好處的便使他們得到好處；這不就是給人民好處，自己卻不耗費嗎？選擇可以勞動的（時間、地點和對象）再去叫他們勞動，又有誰會怨恨呢？自己想要仁德便得到仁德，還貪求什么呢？無論人多人少，無論勢力大小，君子都不敢怠慢，這不是矜持安寧而不驕傲嗎？君子衣冠整齊，目不邪視，態度莊重，使人望見有所畏懼，這不是有威嚴卻不兇猛嗎？"

子張說："四種惡政又是什麼呢？"

孔子說："不先教育便加殺戮叫做虐；不先告誡便求有成績叫做暴；下達可以緩慢執行的命令，而突然要求限期完成叫做賊；同是給人財物，出手吝嗇，叫做小氣。"

20·3 孔子曰："不知命，無以爲君子也；不知禮，無以立也；不知言，無以知人也。"

【譯文】孔子說："不懂得命運，沒有辦法做君子；不懂得禮節，沒有辦法立足於社會；不善於分析人家的言論，沒辦法瞭解人。"

only such tasks as they are capable of performing, is he not laying tasks on them without arousing their resentment? If his desires are set on human-heartedness and he gets it, who can say that he is covetous? Whether a superior man has to deal many people or few, or with things great or small, he dares not slight them: is not this manitaining a dignified ease without any pride? A superior man straightens his robe and hat, and imparts a dignity into his looks, so that, thus dignified, men look up to him with awe: is not this inspiring awe without fierce?"

Zizhang asked, "What are the four vices?"

The Master said, "To put the people to death without having instructed them, this is called cruelty. To require from them the completion of tasks without giving them due warning, this is called oppression. To give careless orders, and be strict when the day comes, this is called robbery. And to be stingy in paying or rewarding men is called littleness."

20.3 Confucius said, "He who does not know the will of Heaven cannot be regarded as a superior man. He who does not know the rules of propriety cannot take his stand. He who does not know words cannot know people."

圖書在版編目（CIP）數據

論語今譯:漢英對照/楊伯峻,吴樹平今譯;潘富恩,温少霞英譯.—濟南:齊魯書社,1993.3(2008.2重印)
ISBN 978-7-5333-0283-2

Ⅰ.論… Ⅱ.①楊…②吴…③潘…④温… Ⅲ.①儒家②論語-譯文-漢、英 Ⅳ.B222.24

中國版本圖書館CIP數據核字（2008）第013417號

論 語 今 譯
（漢英對照）
今譯 楊伯峻 吴樹平
英譯 潘富恩 温少霞
齊魯書社出版發行
（地址:濟南經九路勝利大街39號 郵編:250001）
http://www.qlss.com.cn
E-mail:qlss@sdpress.com.cn
日照報業印刷有限公司印刷
850×1168毫米 32開本 8.25印張 5插頁 196千字
1993年3月第1版 2008年2月第4次印刷
ISBN 978-7-5333-0283-2
定價:17.00圓